WRITING
FOR
MAGAZINES

To Jim

WRITING FOR MAGAZINES

Jill Dick

A & C Black · London

First published 1994
A & C Black (Publishers) Limited
35 Bedford Row, London WC1R 4JH

ISBN 0–7136–3850–8

A CIP catalogue record for this book
is available from the British Library

Cover illustration by Conny Jude

Typeset in 11/12pt Palatino by Florencetype Ltd, Kewstoke, Avon
Printed in Great Britain by Biddles Ltd, Guildford, Surrey

Contents

Introduction

If you want to write for magazines, you'll find all the help and information you need in this book. It's not about fiction or the make-believe items editors sometimes put in to blur the sharp edges of the real world. Here we deal with that very-much-larger piece of the editorial cake: non-fiction. And what an enormous slice of life it covers.

In literally *thousands* of different magazines published weekly, monthly or quarterly, articles appear on almost every conceivable subject, written to appeal to just about everybody. That means people with infinitely varying interests, from all backgrounds, of all ages and every level of education – or none; the intellectual and the man-in-the-street: you, me and the next person you set eyes on. The world and its oyster are the really important people in this book. To the magazine world they are simply 'the readers'. They are the people you will be writing for.

There is so much to write about in so many different ways it's no wonder we writers are always busy. Modern systems of communication bring international events, domestic issues and every concept of life right into our homes; it is easy to be alive to everything happening around us. Most importantly for writers, there is a new freedom to *speak* and that means freedom to write. Regardless of who you are or any actual (or imaginary) handicaps, you can see your work published in the pages of magazines. This sort of writing is simply a craft and like any other craft it can be learned, with perseverance and discipline. Only recently I heard of a respected Bolivian brain surgeon who stunned guests at his retirement party by announcing that he had no medical qualifications whatever. 'Actually,' he said mildly, 'I learned it all from reading books. I am a carpenter by trade.'

Almost anyone can write for magazines, and it makes no difference whether you are male or female (throughout this book 'he' also means 'she' as there is no multi-gender pronoun available). The people who do so without going into regular office jobs are freelances and they were all untrained beginners at one time. They learned how magazines are put together, what editors want and, most importantly, how to provide it. Freelances sell their work to whichever magazines they choose to write for, run their affairs as a part-time hobby or as a small business – and you can do the same.

As if the colossal article field weren't enough, there are many other outlets for non-fiction writers. You may enjoy interviewing, compiling competitions or covering arts events for local and regional magazines. Perhaps you long to run a regular children's page or a gardening column. Writing fillers or letters to the editor may be your strength. Besides the large number of magazines published in the UK each year, a great many more published in America and other English-speaking countries are also wide open to freelance writers. Not only is there an abundance of topics to write about – there is also no shortage of places to sell what you write.

You'll soon grow used to writers' jargon so don't be deterred by the word 'stories' in a book about non-fiction. Any written item or piece of work is referred to as a 'story' in the magazine world. The one thing it never refers to in this book is a fictional or make-believe story. Likewise the word 'copy' simply means any matter eventually to be set in type ready for printing. So anything written, whether typed, word-processed or even hand-written (for letters to the editor) is simply 'copy'.

If the urge to write is strong enough you will already be a writer at heart, even if you have yet to see your work in print. But I do remind you that to achieve publication, especially regularly, demands more than a heart-felt desire, however burning: a great deal more. There are many other people competing against you – including some who have worked on the staff of magazines – and there will be days when all your hard work will seem fruitless. You may wonder whether it is worth going on. 'The artistic temperament is a disease that afflicts amateurs', said G.K. Chesterton, and he certainly knew that writing was hard work. While mere dabbling will get you nowhere worthwhile, achieving publication is incredibly invigorating.

Freelance writing for magazines is exciting, absorbing, and – I can't deny it – sometimes frustrating. But I've never forgotten sitting in an aeroplane beside a party of young girls all clutching copies of a particular magazine just bought in the airport bookshop. The cover told me to watch carefully as they turned the pages – yes! – to an article they pored over before starting an animated discussion about it. You've guessed, of course. They never knew the writer of that article was sitting a few seats away as they reread it and, I'm glad to say, praised it.

Sample that exhilaration and I promise that even when you're an old hand at writing for magazines, with countless published articles to your credit, it never diminishes.

If you persist and achieve your objectives you will know you are really a writer in more than just your heart. And if you are one of the very few as yet untried beginners who meet with instant and sustained success without help from this book or any other source – please write and tell me. I don't often have the chance to shake the hand of genius.

This book is different from others about writing for magazines. It covers everything you need to know in practical terms, and all the information in it is as up to date as possible at the time of going to press. You'll learn how to sell what you write *before* you write it, how to use the same basic material for different magazines – and a great deal more. But it goes further than that. It adds up to a recipe for success, with pages of inside information, that makes the difference between triumph and failure.

On top of that, you'll absorb the most valuable ingredient of all. I can only call it *writing with the professional touch.*

Jill Dick

1
Then and now

This is a book about writing for magazines, not only the ones you see on newsagents' shelves but also the many others regularly published but not so frequently displayed. Do you know there are an estimated 10,000 separate magazines published in the UK alone every year? With most issued either weekly or monthly (and many more published at less frequent intervals) that makes more than *300,000* editions to fill.

Do *you* want to help fill them? If you do, you need only learn what thousands of other magazine writers have already learned – and you will be welcomed with opened arms. The contributor an editor longs to hear from identifies with readers, understands what they want, doesn't patronise or belittle them, feeds them with new ideas and leaves them feeling happier with themselves and their way of life than they were before they bought the magazine. Such a contributor, I need hardly add, is never out of work, is endlessly interested in life and enjoys great personal fulfilment.

On the right lines

The spread of magazine-readership, at one time greatly restricted by the problems of distribution over long distances, increased enormously in the nineteenth century.

Much of this important growth was due to the development of the railways. The first W.H. Smith bookstall was opened at Euston station in 1848 and attracted eager customers among the educated and leisured classes. Twenty-two years later came the Education Act which vastly extended the prospects of reading (and writing) among the majority of the population who had previously been denied such opportunities. Publishing magazines began to be big business. Not without considerable objections and arguments from the railway companies in the early years, stalls selling magazines and periodicals became familiar sights on railway stations in England and Wales.

Trains attracted crowds of people: people not necessarily intending to buy reading material but presenting newsagents with an easy target. By the first years of the new century W.H. Smith had set up more than 140 bookstalls at stations or on the paths leading to them. In Scotland John Menzies, an Edinburgh bookseller, had already branched out into magazine distribution, joined the Scottish Central Railway Company and opened the first of a rapidly expanding string of bookstalls, eventually also taking over Wymans. Countrywide, railway travellers were delighted – and there were further welcome benefits in store for the magazine business.

Titles published before this time had been subject to a hefty tax on all advertisements carried in their pages – which made many of them expensive and therefore limited in their appeal. A high proportion of the general public who could read and desperately wanted to read magazines could not afford to do so. In 1855 Palmerston's government had bowed to the complaints about the so-called 'Taxes on Knowledge' and abolished the stamp duty on newspapers and magazines. At last the way was open and the elements were in place for a surge in the world of magazines: improved transport, particularly the railways, enabled the faster distribution of raw materials and printed matter, while a great new reading public was waiting to buy the results in quantity. Periodical publishing meant business as never before – and it was all going to be in the teeth of stiff competition.

History's helping hands

Some big names dominated the scene during the first half of this century; names that may bring a nostalgic sigh (or perhaps a muttered curse) from older readers of this book. George Newnes, Alfred Harmsworth, C. Arthur Pearson, Amalgamated Press, Odhams, Hulton, Fleetway and the apparently immortal D.C. Thomson of Dundee. Dramatic improvements in printing techniques added strength to publishing empires as well as income to their pockets.

By the early 1930s so great were the numbers of readers claimed by rival magazines and publishing companies that the first Audit Bureau of Circulation began its work. It continues to this day although in substantially changed form as may be expected with the passing of the years.

With huge rises in overall sales the need to effect some assessment of readers became paramount; advertisers as well as publishers had to be sure their wares were reaching their intended destinations and that the money spent in buying advertising space in magazine pages was not being wasted. Whether they knew or cared about it, readers had to be put into fairly rigorous classes to assess their buying propensities. Reader-classification was essential.

Surviving change

Britain was at war in 1939 and many magazines were among the domestic casualties as paper was rationed and staffing levels were reduced. But a surprising number of titles survived and some even flourished. Getting anything to read was difficult and magazines, particularly women's magazines, were passed from hand to hand until they literally fell apart. Restrictions continued for some years after the war ended and by the time they were relaxed many owners and publishers realised the market had changed a great deal. But only 25–30 leading weekly and monthly titles were regularly published. There was a challenging and vigorous optimism in the air and it would not wait; behind it was a new sort of reader – and that classification embraced virtually everybody. The door was wide open for new enterprise and initiative.

Suddenly it seemed that change and the ability to keep pace with it spelt the difference between success and failure for every publisher. While there had always been competition, never was it so cut-throat, with many titles born to short lives after expensive agonies of birth. And another major event altered the nation's social life and imposed new demands on the hard-working magazine business. Commercial television came to snatch mouthfuls of advertising revenue from the hands of periodical publishers; as wounding a stab in the heart of the industry as anyone could have forecast at the time.

More big groups were formed on the basis that unity was strength and made the best use of printing costs, distribution channels, advertising and sales techniques. Magazines appeared for sale in places where they had not been seen before: in the 1960s Canadian Roy Thomson (quite different from the Dundee firm of D.C. Thomson) saw the potential profit of selling food and domestic titles in supermarkets where their tempting glossy covers would attract the eyes of housewives waiting at the checkouts. Racks of magazines appeared at airports, in exhibition foyers, and even on buses in a few lowly populated areas. International publications, mainly originating in the United States, sold like hot cakes in the UK. There was a surging teenage market (as a result of the 'baby boom' after the war) and everywhere publishers, owners, advertisers, distributors, editors and all their staff worked as never before to capture readers and survive. It was simply a question of work hard or collapse – and many collapsed.

Welcome, strangers

With a gruelling pace and survival so uncertain you may wonder why anyone works in the magazine industry at all. Since my own early baptism in it I've seen it as a drug – as writing of any sort is a drug. Affliction is not confined to any particular country and in the 1980s yet another new development gave established publishers here a jolt. European publishers moved in. The immensely resourceful German company Gruner & Jahr had bought the overseas rights to the American magazine *Parents* and were franchising it to several countries in Europe, including Britain. Later they launched *Prima* and then *Best*. Bauer, another German publisher and the largest in the country, immediately launched *Bella*. Marshall Cavendish, publishers of a series of partwork magazines for many years, began publishing partworks for readers to buy week after week or month after month to form their own 'partworks-reference-book' – far better than just a single title – usually covering topics of greater substance in more worthwhile depth. Other titles appeared in English from backgrounds not just in America, but France, Spain, Holland, Italy, Australia . . .

Magazine publishing in this country would never be quite the same again.

Today's magazine scene

It is increasingly difficult to make a precise and tidy categorisation of magazines. In some fields there are many in outright competition with each other, other topics may spawn just one or two titles and a few magazines seem to reign supreme and be acknowledged spokesmen for their particular subjects. It is not even possible to state with accuracy how many titles are published at any one time as new ones are launched and old ones (sometimes not-so-old or even recently launched) close at alarming speed. But it is comforting to know there are more published now than ever before, following a huge rise in numbers in the 1980s and early 1990s – notwithstanding those that have fallen by the wayside in that time. Even at the worst of the recession more magazines were being launched than closed. Media experts predict even stronger growth in magazine publishing in the years ahead; for the majority of us life is becoming more domestic and personal, leading to the prospect of an increasing proportion of published titles designed to satisfy small target groups of buyers. However many titles there are published now and wherever they may be found, between them they cover all the interests of every potential reader. (At first I wrote *virtually* all', but since I have delved more deeply than ever before into the world of magazines for the purposes of writing this book I have no hesitation in stating they cover *everybody*'s interests.)

As well as those listed in reference books there are several hundred more titles that do not feature in any published guides. These may, for example, be magazines covering the interests of specialist groups, 'private' company publications, hobby titles published by and for enthusiasts, charity newsletters, small-press productions and titles published at irregular intervals, perhaps only for particular purposes.

Often the best place to find the answer to a problem is to consult the trade itself, and for writers there are several regularly published guides itemising markets, with details about where to find them, as well as that vital information – what their editors want to buy. There are some 5000 consumer magazines currently published. They are so called because they are 'consumed', i.e. bought, in quantity at regular intervals by the general public. In other spheres such as the food business marketing men refer to items as 'fmcg' – fast-moving consumer goods. A further 2500 periodicals come under the 'business and professional' umbrella and the smaller magazines that do not fall into either of these categories are simply *uncountable*.

Market study isn't just a case of studying the finished product: keeping tabs on who has gone where (and taken personal likes and dislikes to a new market) is also an important part of the job. Like the rest of us, magazine personnel work in a constantly changing employment environment; when your favourite editors (i.e. those who favour *you*) go to edit a magazine somewhere else it often pays to follow them. The good news among this confusion of sorting out what magazines exist is that the large majority welcome freelance submissions while many rely heavily on usable copy from outsiders and some could not survive without it.

Advertising is big business

Now, as in earlier years, the value of studying magazine advertisements cannot be over-emphasised. Whether studying magazines as a potential contributor or merely browsing as a casual reader, never underestimate their power.

Revenue from advertising accounts for more than half the income of consumer magazines. The advertisers rent pages in one or more issues and use the space to sell their own products to readers. Of course those products will be in keeping with the topics covered in the magazine and the obvious predilections of its buyers. It's a matter of horses for courses. Mothers with small babies who buy *Mother & Baby*, for example, are likely to be interested in items of babywear; no advertiser would choose such a market for advertising, say, golfing equipment. That would go in periodicals specifically aimed at and bought by golfers.

So if a close study of advertisements is invaluable, how is the freelance to interpret what they tell us? Advertising agencies know exactly where we readers fit into today's society. Their business success depends on making accurate judgements about who the readers of any given title will be – and writers can learn a good deal from their judgements. The advertisements they place will reflect precisely defined socio-economic categories – that 'reader-classification' mentioned above. Of course not all readers fall into the same group in every respect so even the best advertising agencies do not please everyone all the time – but it is foolish to ignore the benefits their expert studies can offer us.

These socio-economic groups are referred to as A, B, C1, C2, D and E and everyone falls into the appropriate category by a practical evaluation of many factors, some of which may change over the years and cause us to 'move' from one group to another. Among the circumstances deciding our place in the classification are age, occupation, education (our own and our children's), background, the type of house we live in, the car we drive and the holidays we choose. It all adds up to an analysis of our income, capital and, most importantly, our spending power. Did you realise such a ruthless cold-blooded assessment of us and our habits was at work? Rest assured there is nothing sinister in it and everything advertising agencies discover about us is already well documented elsewhere (some of it in the records of the Inland Revenue, alas).

Follow your heart *and* your head

In the very beginning of your market study the task of identifying suitable magazines will usually come second in importance to what you want to write about – and that is the way it should be. Success is most likely to come to those who *enjoy* their work, especially early in their careers. Later, with mounting experience, you will begin to learn what is probably a more professional attitude to writing: to enjoy it in a different sense. To equate 'success' with the fees received for a piece of work, its prominence and importance in its published venue – *and* the pleasure you have had in writing it – to 'enjoy' your work in that sense marks your real progress as a published writer. By then you will have learned that whatever you choose to write simply because it will earn you a good cheque will set you a welcome challenge. It will not be anything to feel embarrassed or guilty about: far from it – it's a challenge you'll have great fun in meeting and a fine sense of achievement in overcoming.

Are you ready?

But we are jumping ahead. Learning to walk before we can run is relevant to writing skills as well as legs. In this book there is help in finding **ideas** to develop for yourself (more usable ones than you can use in a lifetime) and wads of **marketing** information on how to sell your work and do the **research** necessary to give it substance and strength, as well as the essential ingredients of **style** and **structure**.

The special skill of **interviewing** is explored in depth, those niggling questions of how to **present** and despatch your work to editors are simply explained and – for when you want to stretch your talents beyond the writing of articles – a variety of **other writing** outlets is also discussed. Another chapter on marketing extends to selling work **overseas,** how to supply **pictures** to illustrate your articles is fully investigated and in case you still have **problems** some of the more common difficulties (as well as a few occurring less frequently) are given special attention.

The **business** side of writing may not sound exciting but is crucial to success. All you need to know is revealed: how editors think, whether to send query letters or not, how to get commissioned work, your rights in what you have written, discussing fees, keeping records, claiming expenses, paying tax (ugh), syndication, training for the job – and many other useful and important business matters.

2
Ideas

Which comes first, the chicken or the egg; in writing parlance, the idea or the market? This is a teaser much discussed by writers and long ago I found the answer depends on two main components. They are (1) your level of experience in writing and selling, and (2) how well you and your intended market know each other. There are other considerations, of course, which lead some writers to vow getting the idea leads to the market – while others insist the reverse is true.

To hear other writers' opinions I queried magazine writers of varied experience and achievement who agreed to share their views with me and readers of this book. I asked them what they felt should come first – an idea, a market, or anything else – and why. This is what I found:

Most of the beginners or near-beginners put their priorities firmly on ideas and then thought of where to sell, while a few claimed they never had any worthwhile ideas without looking at magazines first.

I defined a success rate of 40 per cent (i.e. acceptance of at least 40 per cent of stories submitted) as 'getting-established', and the majority of those in this category stated finding the markets should come before any writing was done at all. A couple liked to keep the two balls of markets and ideas juggling in the air at the same time, not insisting either was more important than the other.

The last group I queried were more experienced than the others, being former magazine staffers, although their staff jobs did not involve writing. Half admitted to earning 'enough to live on' (their quotes), some were happy with 'satisfactory part-time earnings' and the others didn't reveal their success in money terms. All stressed how hard they worked for their rewards – 'harder than beginners ever appreciate' they said – and two considered marketing had grown so difficult in the recession they were thinking of giving up if the situation didn't improve. Regarding the chicken/egg position they were unanimous: *of course* finding the market comes first. So much for the voice of experience: it is one we would all do well to heed.

As for my second point about how well you and your intended market know each other – that can be of prime importance. Once you have made a few sales to a particular magazine the editor will get to know the type of copy (written work) you can supply, the speed at which you can or will work and – most importantly of all, perhaps – your reliability. No longer will you be starting from scratch with an unknown editor of an unfamiliar market: the stakes will be weighed in your favour. But beware! Complacency loses sales and, although you can feel more comfortable in your relationship with the editor when you have already contributed to the magazine, try sending work that is below the standard required and you'll be rejected as quickly as any raw beginner submitting unsuitable copy.

Getting ideas

Writers without ideas are stuck in sterility: you can't get your mind working, let alone your typing fingers. A few writers claim the mere act of typing throws up ideas but all it does for others is type jumble. With an active and open mind you will never be short of ideas – indeed you will have more than you will ever be able to use. Study every bit of written material you spot: newspapers, magazines, posters, leaflets, announcements, lists of facts and figures, appeals – anything and everything. Listen to radio and watch television with your idea-finding senses on full alert. And don't be embarrassed about listening to other people when they are talking to each other and paying no attention to you. Eavesdrop on conversations in railway carriages or shopping queues or anywhere where people talk. Listen, let your thoughts wander and train them to throw up useful ideas worth working on.

Ponder on snippets: more people in this country are born in May than in any other single month, the dis/advantages of owning your own caravan, regularising the date of Easter, every year more than 50,000 teenage girls become pregnant in Britain and one-third of this number have abortions, the fortieth anniversary of Britain's first commercial television broadcasting,[1] local rags-to-riches stories, house conversions

[1] 22 September 1955.

that went wrong, new ways to use spring vegetables, amateur theatre has more devotees than football . . .

It's just a matter of being on automatic alert: noting all that happens, thinking backwards – and forwards, seeing and hearing through new eyes and ears. What gladdens or saddens, interests or reassures, consoles or explains, intrigues or inspires? To help germination take place ask yourself searching questions: why? who? what? where? when? and how? Twist the questions round too: why didn't? when did? what if?

Topicality and timing

Submitting to a magazine at the right time often makes the difference between success and failure. But don't get caught in the time trap.

The business of magazine publishing is highly organised and falls into several clearly defined parts. There is a great deal of work to be done between editorial planning for edition X and the final appearance of edition X on the bookstalls. Magazines take time to assemble before even reaching the printing stage. Those published every month generally work on a three-month schedule something like this:

For an edition to be published at (say) the beginning of May, go back three months to the start of February. This is the month in which the May issue will be planned and articles will be allotted space, along with everything else that will go into the May pages. Every section of planning each issue must work to set timing because the printers in the composing room, for instance, will almost certainly handle a number of different magazines and each will be booked in for a set period. But the buying, i.e. acceptance of freelance submissions, will already have taken place before this – say during January. So for your article to stand the best chance of appearing in the May edition, from the timing viewpoint alone, it should be on the editor's desk not later than early to mid-January. For Christmas issues your copy (particularly if unsolicited) should be comfortably placed before editors by late June (you can afford to delay a further month or so if not 'going in cold') when some of their December editions will already have been tentatively laid out.

This time-lag between the conception of a particular issue and its eventual publication is called 'lead time' and if you're hoping to sell your copy for a special edition, for instance at the time of the Olympic Games or a Royal event, be sure to give yourself an extra few weeks on top of the magazine's usual lead time. Despite all advice you may find lead time varies between publications and that even those published monthly, for example, work to varying schedules. In general consider a well-established monthly to have a lead time of at least three months, probably four and possibly six. Lead times are reduced for weekly periodicals but the same principle obtains – and for *all* titles the lead time can be ascertained by a simple enquiry.

Have 'timed' copy ready for anything that definitely will happen or is most likely to happen. Whether it be a Royal event (even a death) or the opening of the Channel Tunnel, you can have done all the work and be ready to submit your copy while other writers are still thinking about how to collect the facts. A steady stream of articles is sent by hopeful writers on famous anniversaries and at times of seasonal celebration, so if you plan to join the throng you must think of an unusual aspect of the subject and give it something very special to make an anniversary-weary editor feel life is still worth living.

Many magazines publish regular pieces of anniversary nostalgia with such titles as 'Fifty years ago' or 'This month in (then follows a particular year)'. These are satisfactory pieces to write and, if you have access to a store of early records or old editions of the magazine itself, you can easily write short items on a wide variety of themes to please everyone.

Regular events and anniversaries are good triggers for topical articles but the link between the date (or person, or event) must be strong for your article to stand a chance. Ask yourself 'Why should an editor want this *now*?' and 'Why should he buy *my* article rather than someone else's about this topic?' If you can't find good answers to both questions he probably won't.

What do you know?

Your own experience of life is a valuable source of ideas with the advantage you will certainly be able to write with authority. Give yourself the exercise of reflecting on what you did yesterday and make a list of a dozen ideas your activities suggested. Can you do that? For instance, it may be impossible to find a particular toy currently popular with children, so you make one out of papier-mâché. Written with specific instructions and diagrams this could find a ready audience in the right magazine. Perhaps your bike broke down and you fixed it; other bikers face this problem and many don't know how to fix it. Your friends running small businesses may provide you with ideas by their very enterprise. Two 40+ sisters in my village were facing early retirement, which neither wanted, and set up in business cleaning out people's wheelie bins after the council emptied them every week. Clad in hygienic face masks, red bobble hats and *white* boiler-suits, they wielded high-pressure hoses as if born to the job – and many were the encouraging smiles received from grateful customers when 'Bill and Ben, the wheelie-clean men' doffed their masks and hats. That made such a good story for a local magazine the editor was pleased to be giving the wheelie-clean 'men' free publicity, and me a good fee. Naturally I didn't let it rest there as this was certainly a story for a larger audience . . .

Women's magazines often want 'What happened to me' stories – frequently accompanied by pictures. Not long ago I talked to a woman whose three-year-old daughter had been marooned in a burning building. As she and her husband were held back by firemen they (and other people on the ground) saw a young woman appear at an upstairs window. She shouted to the firemen and threw down the child – who was caught uninjured. The parents swore there was nobody else in the house at the time, that they had never seen the young woman before and had no idea how she came to be in their house to save their daughter's life. In due course the firemen put out the fire. They found no body but among the burned timbers of the child's bedroom they did find a gold bracelet which they returned to the child's parents. They had never seen it before. This was, of course, a true story but not until it was published in a women's magazine was the mother able to – I can't say 'finish it' so much as 'add another twist to it'. The week after publication a young man identified the bracelet. He had given it to his girlfriend soon after she discovered she would never be able to bear a child, but she had scorned it and walked out on him. He had not seen her since and had assumed she had left the neighbourhood.

Does an unfinished story intrigue you as it does me? I checked all the authorities I could find but discovered no trace of any girl reported missing and there has been no further development of the story as I write this.

As the chapter on market study will remind you, be careful when writing about your own affairs. There are magazines welcoming nostalgia or personal opinions but writing about something too close to your heart in a market not wanting either will kill your story. Another risk in writing about what you know (advice regularly offered to beginners without this warning) is that being so close to your subject you may find it hard or even impossible to explain it to readers new to the subject. Writers of computer manuals regularly fall into this trap: many a manual designed for newcomers to computing is nigh incomprehensible until a friend has explained it in non-technical terms – and then you understand it and barely need the manual anyway. So be careful you don't assume readers have as much knowledge of your pet subject as you have – or veer too far the other way and think their ignorance of it makes them idiots.

In truth everything you have ever known or thought or felt or witnessed or heard or read or wanted or feared or dreamed about (or eaten, suffered, enjoyed – the list is endless) is material in which ideas are found. A fertile imagination responds well to exercise and soon you'll find you have more than enough to write about – of the right sort.

Ideas from ads and pix

Advertisements and pictures (ads and pix, as journalists call them) provide useful source material for idea-hunters. To hit the nail right on the head, in terms of what the ad is trying to sell, is what advertising copy-writers are paid for. The most successful ads incorporate a good idea just as do the most successful articles. The long-running television commercials for a certain brand of coffee spawned a light romantic story carried beyond the television screen into magazines and newspapers – because viewers grew to care, not so much about the quality of the coffee, but about a good-looking actor and actress who managed to turn every occasion into one for drinking coffee. Viewers are also magazine readers so clever writers were quick to exploit what appealed to public imagination.

Look at pictures in a new light: not only advertising pix but also others in public places, on magazine or newspaper pages, on television – anywhere and everywhere. Browsing on newsagents' shelves isn't only useful when you're looking for markets to write for; a quick flip through published copies of those potential markets can prove valuable in giving you ideas about what to write. Sometimes it can also surprise you. Finding a feature on the very topic you have in the back of your mind may not be welcome but at least it will save you time and effort in what would probably have been wasted research for that market.

An unlimited source

Look at any dictionary of dates and you'll be bursting with ideas before reaching the second page. Here are anniversaries by the thousand covering events in countless spheres: entertainment, politics, royalty, shipwrecks, music, battles – anything you care to name will have anniversaries editors will buy. Opened at random *Chambers Dates* tells me 6 May 1994 will be the fortieth anniversary of the day Roger Bannister became the first person to run a mile in less than four minutes. He did it in 3 minutes and 59.4 seconds on the Iffley Road track in Oxford. In August 1936 Elizabeth Cowell made her debut at Alexandra Palace in Muswell Hill, London, as the first woman television announcer. Oliver Cromwell declared England a Commonwealth and abolished the monarchy in March 1649.

Remember the schoolboy who thought history began with William the Conqueror and ended with Queen Victoria? Nobody explained to him that history is what happens today – looked at tomorrow. Events in the recent past are always popular in small localities so articles about local history often sell well in magazines with an area or limited circulation. Let an editor receive an article he knows will evoke responses of 'Ah yes, do you remember . . . ?' from his readers and all else being equal he'll probably buy it.

If you like looking back to make an article for the future, buy a good book of dates, scan the pages of any encyclopaedia or study material published in the area in the recent past. Inspiration won't be long in coming.

A few to get you going . . .

Adopt the habit of idea-thinking everywhere you go and with everything you do. The frogspawn in my pond develops into hundreds of tadpoles, many of which do not survive into baby let along adult frogs. Idea-germination is similarly prolific and at first may seem equally wasteful, but I've often found a tadpole stored away in a forgotten corner of my mind will develop later and become quite a handy frog. A wise man makes more opportunities than he finds (according to Francis Bacon) and mentally nothing is ever wasted. Take a look at these, for instance:

- Mnemonics have been one of my hobbies for many years and I have written many articles on this theme. They intrigue a lot of other people and the more I write about them the more I collect as readers send me their favourites. This is an example of choosing popular subjects to write about – or at least subjects that fall into the 'light amusement' category. Many readers will remember:

  Willy Willy Harry Ste
  Harry Dick John Harry III
  One two three Neds Richard II
  Henry IV V VI – then who?[2]

  but not so well known (and therefore seized upon by enthusiasts) is the order in which Henry VIII married his wives:

  Catherine of Aragon stole a jar of tarragon.
  'It's the last in the bin', she told Anne Boleyn.
  'Give me more!' begged Jane Seymour.
  Which made Anne of Cleeves spill some on her sleeves.
  'Not for me! I'm a coward!' said Catherine Howard.
  But Catherine Parr drank the rest of the jar.

  or (just to show not all mnemonics have royal connections):

  Bless My Dear Aunt Sally[3]

- Vivid dreams do you good. Well, that's an opinion sold to a weekly magazine and supported by carefully researched personal stories.
- 'Cyril came to stay for a month' told the story of a tiny grey squirrel found cowering in a hedge and how we fed him from a baby's bottle until he was big and fit enough to be released into the wild.

[2] You do know the rest . . . er, don't you?
[3] The order of numerical or algebraic expression: brackets, multiplication, division, addition and subtraction.

- Pantomime was never invented – it just grew. This is a fascinating story, particularly at the right time of year.
- A collection of press misprints made hilarious reading in a popular weekly magazine: 'The survey records there are 10,638 people sharing an outside toilet.' 'Photographer will shoot children for Christmas.' 'A body was found in a burnt out hen house on Saturday but police do not suspect foul play.'

  And funny stories written to civil servants: 'I need milk for my baby as her father is unable to supply it.' 'Regarding my dentures, the teeth at the top are good enough but the ones in my bottom hurt me.'
- Listening to a relative's fight to help a family in Mexico gave me the idea for an article about how one small community there copes with trouble.
- The well-loved words about death by Canon Scott Holland can bring comfort to readers of widely different publications: *Death is nothing at all . . . I have only slipped away into the next room . . .* Although we long to help the bereaved, death is still a topic few of us can write about. Can you?

Anyone could fill this book with lists of ideas; maybe some of the above will light a spark in your head, giving birth to an original idea. But nobody else's ideas will be as valuable to you as those you think up for yourself – because they will be *yours*.

Remember, the first glimmering of a general idea is often vague and insubstantial – until it gives way to the particular one unique to *you*. If you feel yourself adrift in an idea-empty sea or an ocean of floating images that don't interconnect, set yourself the task of listing five ideas you think you could write about and do it *now*. Carry your list about with you and study it constantly until you decide which single idea is going to be the first to have your full attention.

Changing and developing ideas

Make many articles out of a single idea. One day I watched a girl in a hairdresser's salon sweeping up bits of hair that had been cut from customers' heads. I wondered how much human hair was thrown away every day throughout the world and how far it would stretch, were it all joined together

in a single thread. Idle musing? Perhaps. But it led to a string
(*sic*) of articles in a variety of magazines on the following
themes:

- Hair care and cleanliness in the eighteenth century. (Some
  of the facts I uncovered were pretty hair-*raising*.)
- Why men make top hairdressers for women.
- Your mirror image: what does it reveal? (Facts and figures
  about left and right handedness.)
- Hair today, why gone tomorrow? (What to do with hair
  we throw away. Suggestions ranged from mixing it with
  tarmac for absorbing rain on roads to composting it into a
  new thatching material vying with straw for the 'natural'
  epithet.)
- Your hair is what you eat. (A diet-for-health piece.)
- Models who never complain. (About dressing the hair of
  dummies in museums, etc.)

Often digging into how you are going to deal with a particular idea throws up what strikes you as a better one. If this
happens (as it frequently does to me) be glad that you're getting two or even more ideas from one and put aside the one(s)
you don't immediately start working on. There is no failure in
changing your mind about what you are going to write as
long as it only happens in private. If you are going to present
your idea rather than the finished article to an editor, you
must be quite sure there is no changing your mind after he's
approved it or agreed you should go ahead with the project.

If one good idea leads to another, as it certainly does, make
sure you don't spend all your time generating ideas, invaluable as they are. Before too long you must make a clear decision about which one you're going to develop next. Only you
have access to those revolving inside your head – and for you
they will be the best.

Well-travelled words

Travel is a field demanding specialist attention but it is not
always as easy as it sounds. Writing articles about your holidays, where you've been, what you've done and seen, interesting people you've met, and so on, can make very worthwhile copy and often sells well. I know several freelance
writers who regularly recoup all they spend on holidays

by writing about them. Some go further and make a point of lining up possible markets whenever they travel anywhere – on business, for family reasons or for their own relaxation. A large number of magazines publish copy about travel for readers who simply want to know about places they've heard of or read about and might like to see for themselves. Magazine-wise they are potential tourists rather than travellers.

Wherever we writers go, within these shores or overseas, we can always take an unusual viewpoint, find a fascinating person, reveal little-known information or offer practical advice to others following in our footsteps. A place that is familiar to you, because you've been there before, will be excitingly original for countless readers who haven't. It's your job as a 'tourist' writer to give them a taste for it. Tempt them with the flavour, encourage them with descriptive and imaginative language and resolve their doubts with solid facts and figures about getting there, details of where they can stay, the currency, any paperwork or special health regulations involved and anything else they would want to ask if you were telling them of your experiences face to face.

Being a 'travel writer' is rather different, particularly in the eyes of most glossy publications. Those existing solely as travel rather than general or other-topic magazines frequently complain at receiving too many mundane accounts of people's holidays. Their editors seldom accept unsolicited copy and all work is either directly commissioned or at least arranged after detailed consultation. For the cover prices they charge, the quality of the advertisements they attract and the 'travel professionalism' their readers expect, only the best will do. With high standards to maintain they will even reject copy already invited (which is not the same as commissioned) if it fails to evoke in readers the essential 'feeling' of the place visited. Here again, study of the market is particularly important as the magazines wanting travel articles vary greatly in their levels of sophistication.

A most useful book on the subject is:

Writing about Travel by Morag Campbell. A. & C. Black, 35 Bedford Row, London WC1R 4JH. Tel: 071–242 0946.
The author was for many years editor of *Signature*, the Diners Club magazine, which involved the commissioning

of travel articles. Having travelled the world and contributed travel articles to countless publications she
includes every aspect of the job. £5.95.

If you live in or near London you may also find **The Travel
Bookshop**, 13 Blenheim Crescent, London W11 2EE (Tel:
071–229 5260) well worth a visit.

Borrowing, copying or stealing?

On the principle that there is nothing new in the universe,
decide to write about, for instance, pollution in Britain and of
course you won't be the first person to do so. But you are not
guilty of borrowing, copying or stealing someone else's idea.
What matters is the imagination and enthusiasm the idea
plants in your head, coupled with your unique way of writing about it. The ideas in a previous section may be no help
to you because they ignite no spark; if that is so, it is because
they are not *your* ideas. Use other people's to find your own,
to set you reflecting, contrasting, developing and generally
giving your imagination room to expand in the way only you
can. When I first understood what pundits meant by such
'lateral thinking' I realised I had been doing it instinctively all
my life. Ideas float about by the million but the best *for you*
are fed by a natural individuality that will show through the
written words and breathe life into your work.

Testing ideas

To test ideas objectively I let them lie fallow for a while. When
I look at them again I am no longer blinded by what seemed
a brilliant conception and can ask myself some rigorous questions. The first – will this idea be of sufficient interest to
editors and readers? – will be answered by detailed market
study (see the next chapter) but even before that I must ask
'Do I have or can I obtain all the information I'm going to
need to develop the idea?' Only if the answer is 'Yes' can I go
ahead with any degree of hope (I almost said 'confidence' but
that might be a little too optimistic at this stage of the article-
planning process).

Later in this book you will find details of how to set about
the research work required to put backbone and credibility
into articles. It is a comfort to know experts in research have

gone before us and can put us on the right track in that vital aspect of writing.

Knowing or assembling facts and figures needed for the task is one thing: assessing whether you have enough may be quite another. Everything we write is more convincing when we know a great deal more 'behind the scenes' than we need to reveal to the reader. Such extra knowledge adds a certain authority and reliability to our work which reassures the reader that we really do know what we're writing about.

So an idea must be followed by the initial finding of at least the important facts to support it before a judgement can be made about its viability. Never fall into the trap of trying to clothe an idea, particularly what might otherwise have been a good one, in costume so scanty it won't keep out cold editorial condemnation. Trying to spread the sparse covering further than it will go only leads what's underneath to a quicker death.

A different test to subject your ideas to concerns pictures. Will the resultant article(s) need them, or be more likely to sell with them? Chapter 11 deals with this aspect of article-submission but before you begin writing you need to answer 'Will I need pix?' And if the answer is 'Yes', can you acquire them?

Keeping an ideas file

When your head is crammed with ideas and you are sur-rounded by scrappy notes on bits of paper, it is time to sort them into files. Mine are usually concertina-type cardboard files in which I store items of idea-generating information usually in the form of clips and cuttings I find here and there. As you look out for ideas you should also watch for cuttings: bits out of newspapers or magazines you might find useful. Be sure to check what your cuttings tell you (could the writer be wrong?) and always date them.

Most writers carry notepads all the time. Some paper, a pen and a little pair of folding scissors can work wonders for your storage files. (I hope my dentist isn't reading this but I'm always glad to be left alone in the waiting room as he has a lively supply of magazines on the table . . .) Look upon ideas as not only necessary to work on now, but also as your stock in trade for a rainy day in the future.

I confess I've often found it easier to write about a fixed

subject than pluck one out of the air. If an editor indicates he wants an article about Jimi Hendrix or whether ballpoint pens are biodegradable, you may breathe a sigh of relief that the topic itself indicates the route you must follow to complete the task. There will be no problem of finding an idea or worrying about whether you can or can't support it with all the necessary facts and figures. Meanwhile you'll have a pleasant surprise the next time you glance at the bulging ideas file you are constantly adding to. With all those ideas of your own jostling for your attention, idea-finding will never be a problem again.

3
Markets

Finding markets is not difficult. Take a careful look at the magazine racks next time you're in a newsagent's shop; not as a casual buyer, but as a potential contributor. And then remember that even the largest shop with the greatest display area cannot hope to show more than a fraction of the total markets available to writers like us. There are probably some *five* times as many published as any shop can possibly display and it is a fact that most freelance writers ignore four-fifths of the markets that publish freelance work simply because they do not know they exist.

That's encouraging but the difficulty, of course, lies in finding the right market at the right time for the right piece of work written in the right way. Many editors are not only delighted to receive publishable material in their daily postbags, they actually rely on it. So there are magazines wanting *us* as badly as we want *them* – yet still market study can be a jungle. Straightening it out is what this chapter is all about.

What markets exist

New magazines are launched and others die even as I write this, but more than 7000 are listed in the pages of one of the UK's monthly advertising guides (see below) and there are at least 2000 more small magazines and journals that do not carry advertising so do not reach its pages. Simply by keeping our eyes and ears wide open at all times we can find many more that are not listed *anywhere* – for there are always some that never will be. (If this comment makes your sales ear twitch you are made of the right material for a freelance writer: lesser-known markets not advertised to other potential contributors frequently prove to be steady worthwhile buyers.)

Among this super-abundance of magazines for readers to read and writers to contribute to let's take a look at the main publishers of the big consumer titles. No, I'm not suggesting you aim at the most difficult targets if you're at the start of your writing career, but sorting-by-ownership is a logical and valuable way of grouping magazines together.

The first vital statistic is circulation. This proclaims success as nothing else can; glossy covers, stunning publicity, brilliant contents, dedicated editorial work and everything else that goes into a magazine count for naught if the number of copies sold is insufficient to support the cost of production. So circulation is the life-blood of periodicals. Sales are measured by the Audit Bureau of Circulation which reports its findings every six months. You can guess how hard those at the top work to retain their positions and how avidly the half-yearly ABC list is studied.

High on it as I write are many periodicals published by the giant IPC Magazines company owned by Reed International. But even they can't lay claim to first place. The four consumer titles currently selling more than one million copies per issue are *Radio Times, Reader's Digest, TV Times* and *What's on TV*. Does that surprise you? The last two are published by IPC and within the first fifty come their famous five: *Woman's Weekly, Woman's Own, Woman, Woman's Realm* and *Woman & Home*. Other IPC titles lower down the list but still fully viable include *Family Circle, Yachting World, Marie Claire, 19, Horse & Hound* and *Living*.

The other major publishers compete strongly. Argus House concentrates on hobby magazines like *Model Boats* and *Film Monthly*; Condé Nast go for qualities – *House & Garden, Vogue* and *Vanity Fair*, among them. EMAP (East Midlands Allied Press) is the third largest publisher and continues to prosper following the purchase of 26 leading titles from the stable of the late Robert Maxwell in 1992. Their titles include *Here's Health, Fishing News, Which Computer?, Mother & Baby* and *Practical Gardening*. A further hundred or so titles were also bought from the former Maxwell Consumer Publishing & Communications empire by HHL Publications who now issue such diverse titles as *Postman Pat, Wedding & Home* and *Practical Householder*. Link House, Morgan-Grampian and Benn (owned, among others, by the huge United News-papers) boast titles as varied as *The Countryman, Prediction, Hi-Fi News & Record Review, Farming News* and *Pulse*. From Macmillan come mainly medical publications including *Nursing Times*, the National Magazine Company issues *Good*

Housekeeping, Cosmopolitan and *She*, while old-established D.C. Thomson of Dundee concentrates on comics, *Sporting Post* and the ever popular *People's Friend*. G. & J. (Gruner & Jahr) do very well with *Prima*, with sales of 738,000, and *Best* with 658,000.

Not many people know this . . .

Not all magazines open to freelance contributors fall into the 'consumer' bracket and see their circulation figures recorded by the Audit Bureau of Circulation. In a separate category, for assessment purposes, lie the large number of business magazines, whose success is measured by the value of the display advertising carried on their pages. You may be surprised to find which magazines fall into this classification, including some you had hardly thought of as being 'different' from consumer titles on sale to the general public. On the current list of the Media Monitoring Service (the ABC equivalent for business magazines) come *Farmers Weekly, Computer Shopper, Commercial Motor, Music Week* and *Bathrooms*. From the writer's point of view there is virtually no difference between studying the pages of business titles and poring over consumer magazines: if either want freelance contributors, that's the only spur we need. There's just one extra point: I said they are virtually the same but there is one important difference. Because business magazines are less obvious targets freelance writers submitting to their pages often face little competition.

Sorting by appeal

Now we'll look at the types of magazines available. Publications of all sorts fall into specific categories according to the likes and tastes of readers they are designed to capture. In talking about types of magazines we are really referring to the types of readers who (largely without realising it) dictate the content, price, cover, advertisements and editorial slant of every title in the market place.

Understanding, therefore, that magazines are classified according to their potential readers, this is a broad selection of the types available:

animals, birds and fish	literary and fiction
art and antiques	men's interests

business and finance	motoring
buying and selling	music and hi-fi
children and young people	outdoor activities
computers	photography
county and regional	puzzles and crosswords
current and world affairs	sports
electronics	teenage and pop
entertainment	trade and professional
hobbies and pastimes	transport
home and garden	travel
international	women's interests

These are some of the classifications used by newsagents when they have to decide what to display on their shelves. Decisions must be made as space restricts what can be shown in any one shop and each local owner will choose what he thinks is most likely to sell in his area. So don't imagine that titles given the best display positions on your newsagent's shelves necessarily sell the most copies all over the country. A display in the centre of a major city will differ from one in a small county town or another in a rural village. Shops in areas with a high proportion of young people are unlikely to display the same magazines (or even types of magazines) as those where an above-average number of residents are elderly. Remember, too, that newsagents are not the only people to sell magazines. Women's and general magazines are on sale in about 10 per cent of major supermarkets; *Family Circle* and *Living* sell nowhere else.

The likely interests of passing browsers will also affect what is displayed in any shop, and here we meet another large and difficult-to-categorise section of the magazine world – general-interest titles.

'General-interest' is the term used to describe periodicals that appeal to a wide variety of readers who themselves cannot be readily classified. Religion, for instance, and health, and humour are of interest (although they may be of particular appeal to many folk) to people of all levels of intelligence and taste. In the 'general-interest' category you will find magazines such as the following:

Astronomy Now	*Reader's Digest*
Conservation Now	*Royalty Monthly*
Horoscope	*Soldier*

Jewish Chronicle	*Unexplained*
Miniature Wargames	*Yours*

Each classified or general-interest type embraces widely vary-
ing titles. 'Art and antiques', for example, covers *Clocks*, *Be
Creative*, *Leisure Painter* and *Coin News* – four very different
magazines, each with its own individuality and character.
'Children and young people' is broken down into more than
400 (yes, *four hundred*) separate publications ranging from
Sylvanian Family to *Beano* (still going strong) and from *Police
Academy* to *Wonder Woman*.

Take any generic theme and you'll find what is sometimes
a bewildering array of magazines published for its devotees.
'Motoring' supports many different publications, as do
'music' and 'cookery'. In fact it is impossible to think of a
single topic that is not subdivided into a whole range of titles,
so great is the variety and range of readers' interests.

Follow the experts

If classification by the subject matter of a magazine fails to
narrow the field sufficiently for us to study it with meaningful results, let us look at the magazine world through the eyes
of people who depend on it for a living – the publishing companies. You can be sure they know exactly what they're doing
in the business of market study and there is much we can
learn from them. Every issue of every magazine reveals tell-
tale signs of how the market-researchers have done their
work. If they have made a good job of it (and continue to do
so, for it is not a one-off task that can be forgotten when a new
title is launched or an existing one comfortably established)
we do well to study every ingredient of their success. Why do
some titles succeed and others fail? Ask yourself who the
magazine is aimed at. Why should those people buy one
rather than another one in competition to it? Is the 'masthead'
(the title of the magazine usually splashed across the top of
the front cover) clear and bright? Is there a catchy title slogan?
Is the magazine's appeal obvious? A publication without a
clearly defined target is doomed to failure. Are there any
ominous signs (such as editorial gaucherie, shortage of office
staff, constant failure in communication and slow payment)
of impending closure? Magazines fold (the jargon for 'going

bust') in good times as well as bad, and contributors know that being left with copy published but not paid for by a now defunct publishing company is depressing and demoralising.

How *old* are you, gentle reader?

It can never be true to say that once you know about a reader's background and lifestyle you automatically know what he or she would like to read, but there are undoubted clues well worth following. Some are more easily ascertained than others. Test yourself with this as I tell you about Sally Carter. (I hope for the purposes of this little example that you don't happen to know a real Sally Carter: if you do, please substitute another name that will not immediately make you think of anyone in particular, nor put any preconceived ideas into your head about the lady's credentials or personality.)

My Sally has brown hair and is of medium height. She lives in a semi-detached house on the outskirts of London, enjoys meeting her friends for evenings out and is fond of cooking.

Not much individuality has emerged about Sally yet, has it? Tens of thousands of women have brown hair and are of medium height, live just outside London, like cooking – and so on. What single extra scrap of information will give Sally the breath of life in your mind's eye, albeit you and I (and probably Sally too) know she is only make-believe? The colour of her eyes? Her job, if she has one? Her marital state? The last two might offer clues to give her at least a vague outline in your imagination.

But what will tell you more about her than will anything else is her *age*. Let me mention (or let you deduce) that Sally Carter is 40, or collecting her retirement pension, or has three children under five and you will instantly place her in a broad category in your mind. I hope it will be broad too, for – as we all know – there are many people who do not fit into their expected age groups and are sometimes way out of it. But at least you are likely to have the right idea about Sally. As magazine publishers and editors plan their target readership very carefully indeed before launching expensive new titles, they too are looking at the average reader for the age group they hope to reach, rather than those who perversely fall outside it. So, as soon as you know the age or approximate age of a magazine's readers you will have the first overall idea of the sort of people the magazine is hoping to attract.

Given an age range of, say, 18–24 the average age aimed at would be 21 but great care would be taken not to limit or even concentrate the title's appeal to those aged 21. There is no profit in gaining half a dozen new readers by appealing to their exact age group and losing six others by ignoring theirs. Remembering this point, here are the average reader-age ranges of some leading magazines:

Woman's Own	38
House & Garden	43
Cosmopolitan	27
People's Friend	58
She	36
Elle	24
Woman	37
Chat	30
Options	30

If you cannot discover the average reader-age of a particular title despite research and your closest market study, simply contact the magazine and *ask*.

How to study markets

Market study is rather like trying to unbake a cake. There are all the ingredients, mixed to perfection by an expert; to discover the recipe the cake must be *un*baked, i.e. reduced to its constituent parts. But doing that will reveal the ingredients only of that particular cake. And here our allegory ends: many cakes are baked to a single recipe, as we all know, but no periodicals are the same week after week or month after month.

Research into the market guides listed later in this chapter is a beginning and will provide outline information about magazines, but true market study means studying the magazines themselves. There is no substitute for purposeful, thorough and organised appraisal of the contents of your potential market over a period of time. For monthly magazines a study of at least four issues is advisable, including the most recent, and paying close attention to at least six editions of a weekly magazine is likely to yield the best results.

When we've found the magazines we want to write for (or

think we want to write for, as further acquaintance with them might make us change our minds), how do we set about the actual study? To do it at all is important, not so each of us may discover exactly what everyone else studying them discovers, but in order to bring that extra *personal* impression to our minds – so we don't all emerge with identical opinions and subsequently write articles lacking originality. That is also why market study has no hard-and-fast rules but what I will only call guidelines which should be bent and stretched to suit *you*, as an individual writer. You may have read conflicting advice about the whole matter. You may even have heard some writers boast they never bother with it at all; have you also heard about their level of success or failure compared to the number of scripts they submit to editors?

So here are some guidelines, beset with provisos and cautions and let-outs as all such precepts must be when they attempt to govern anything as creative and character-driven as writing:

- Discover what magazines exist for readers who share or might share interest in your chosen topic.
- Buy, beg or borrow as many different magazines on the topic as you can.
- Study them analytically as a writer as well as a reader for insight into editorial aims.
- Make your choice of market (or markets) and stick to your decision – while not closing your mind to future articles along similar or allied lines.
- Keep note of any new ideas born of studying the magazine and set them aside for future development.
- Go back to the first point – and keep going.

I know tutors who advise scrupulous dissection of every word, analysing its place, purpose and effectiveness – until the whole magazine is reduced to a mass of tangled statistics. Frankly, I find this more like character assassination than market study and it kills the very goose I hope is going to nurse my golden egg. To describe a magazine as having character is not foolish sentimentality but a valid assessment of what makes it what it is, just as each of us has a personality different from that of anyone else.

All the same, sensible analysis is important. Take a sheet of paper and write down the number of pages of your chosen magazine, noting what proportion of them is given to advertising, editorial matter (that's everything written in-house by the editor or his staff) and other copy. The last may or may not be written by freelances and regular examination of consecutive issues will often reveal whether particular items are, or were, freelance 'spaces'. Don't be downcast if you cannot at first differentiate between freelance and non-freelance material; this is a skill that greatly improves with practice.

Also note the magazine's price and frequency of publication, both of which give an immediate indication of the readers who are its target. Observe the thickness of the paper, the effectiveness of layout and the quality of the illustrations. All these help to give you a picture of the average reader.

First-person pieces will almost certainly be freelance copy, as will anything temporarily out of the usual style for the magazine you are studying. Provided they have the space and that company policy allows them a degree of flexibility, editors seldom observe rigid terms in how much freelance material they buy. If offered just what they want they eagerly bend any preconceived plans for any particular issue not already advanced beyond the 'no-change' stage. So when your market study tells you magazine X devotes, say, 30 per cent of its content to freelance material and most of that seems to be filled with regular or specialist columns, don't abandon any hopes you may have of submitting to it. If you write what the editor wants, space will always be found. Perhaps that last sentence sums up all we writers need to know.

A good deal of magazine study falls into an observation of the style and structure of its language and how it treats its readers. Never forget what we are really studying is not magazines but *readers*. Are they treated cheerfully, with triviality, as serious-minded thinkers, as if their main concerns are domestic, adventurous, romantic, creative – or how? Is the language used appropriate for immature youngsters, folk with some experience in the topic the magazine deals with or for readers attracted by history and nostalgia? Above all, do *you* know how to talk to them? Picture the very readers the magazine is trying to reach and if possible think of someone you know who might be one.

Don't forget there is an army of PROs (public relations Officers) waiting to help you. It is more precise to say they are waiting to help the company that employs them, which will be the publishing company promoting the magazine, but they can be of great value to writers. Ask for their leaflets on the readership of your chosen magazine, the launch plans (if it is new or about to be launched) and any other relevant material they care to supply. You never know what they might hand out and the more useful information you amass the better.

It is a blessing to have close friends and be able to talk to them freely. They do not necessarily have to agree with you, yet you can confide in them. You don't have to wonder what their reactions will be – you already know because you have an established relationship with them. The most valuable advice anyone can offer in the business of market study is this: get to 'know' the readers as well as you know your friends. Then you will instinctively understand what they do and do not want. And once you understand, you know exactly what to write.

When your copy is published you can't talk to the readers directly or see their reactions to what they read. You get no help from nods and agreement, frowns, 'Ah, this is just what I want', or even 'Rubbish' as your article is thrown down in disgust. You have to judge (or do your best to judge, which is really the most any of us can do) how readers' minds work. That is what communication is all about in any and every type of writing: understanding what goes on in other people's heads and knowing how to get something out of yours into theirs.

Women are special

So far we've looked in several ways at the vast array of magazines we might or could contribute to; from their circulation, their publishers, their types and the ages of their average readers. But there are still some special categories that deserve particular attention for various reasons – and the first covers the huge number of magazines for and about women.

Although you may not particularly want to write for women (at the moment, at least), so overwhelming is the concentration of magazines geared to their interests that you would be distancing yourself from a large and potentially lucrative section of the overall market were you to ignore it. Women buy over 85 per cent of all titles of all types and 'women's interest' titles sell in greater quantities than do those in any other single section of the market. Most importantly for us, editors of these magazines buy a higher proportion of what they print from freelances than do editors of other magazines. No wonder the 'women's interest' titles are almost worth a book in themselves.

The high circulation figures of the leading magazines for women reflect their constant popularity, recession or no recession. These (in round figures) are ten of the current best-sellers:

Woman's Weekly	905,000
Woman's Own	782,000
Prima	738,000
Woman	716,000
Best	658,000
Me	595,000
Chat	556,000
People's Friend	473,000
Cosmopolitan	472,000
My Weekly	459,000

As a matter of interest, *The Lady*, born 1885 and the oldest surviving magazine for women, currently sells 66,000 copies a week.

Take notice of women's magazines and you'll quickly see how widely they vary. Apart from appearing weekly or fortnightly (and occasionally at less frequent intervals) at prices 'to suit all pockets' as they say, the feeling of nearly all – in their various ways – is *uplifting*. The monthlies usually include more in-depth articles than their weekly counterparts simply because there is a longer time between editions in which to get everything done. Usually, if appropriate to the readership, there will be glossy illustrations, a luxurious tone and a relaxed impression of quality. On the whole the doors of these magazines are closely guarded by writers 'in the know' and it is difficult for newcomers to break into their pages, in fact often impossible, without prior contact with the editor. But, as with every publication at every level, those writing for its pages now were at one time unknowns . . .

In this specialised field the many weeklies for women present less experienced freelances with countless opportunities. Of course, close study of what is required is essential. And always remember, particularly at this vibrant but cut-throat level of competing titles, that what you see in the latest issue is what they decided to publish about six weeks ago. Re-reading 'Topicality and timing' in Chapter 2 will refresh your mind about those vital lead times which apply to all periodicals and which, if ignored, can consign to oblivion the brain-child on which you've lavished tender loving care for days or weeks.

Published market guides

There are numerous reference books listing magazines. Some are more detailed than the rest, several reveal information others do not and a few concentrate on specialist magazines for specialist readers (and usually for specialist writers).

All the books referred to below are published regularly and it is important to keep up to date with any study of them. While much of their content may not have changed since publication of the previous edition, parts may be radically different. Consult an out-dated reference book and you could base your work on what is now misleading and useless information. And all wasted effort steals valuable working time. Incidentally, don't waste any looking for some magic comprehensive list. There simply isn't a single reference guide listing *all* periodicals published at the time the guide itself is published.

The following are, in their various ways, invaluable:

Writers' & Artists' Yearbook, A. & C. Black Ltd, 35 Bedford Row, London WC1R 4JH. Tel: 071–242 0946. The most important guide for any writer's bookshelf and the acknowledged leader in its field. It is divided into two main sections of markets and general information. The latter includes guidance on how to submit material, cope with income tax and deal with illustrations, among other useful topics, while the large marketing section lists magazine titles, addresses, cover prices, frequency of publication, rates of pay and brief editorial requirements. £9.99.

Willing's Press Guide, Reed Information Services, Windsor Court, East Grinstead House, East Grinstead, West Sussex RH19 1XA. Tel: 0342 326972.   An alphabetical list detailing about 1000 periodicals. It will prove invaluable although the UK volume alone costs £102. More a book for library consultation than purchase?

BRAD (British Rate & Data), Maclean Hunter Ltd, Maclean Hunter House, Chalk Lane, Cockfosters Road,

Barnet, Herts. EN4 0BU. Known by the acronym BRAD
this is a monthly advertising guide. A massive volume
costing £130 for a single copy or £335 per annum, which
probably also qualifies for library-only consultation, it
currently lists more than 7000 periodicals, all earning their
places solely because they carry advertising material,
which countless smaller publications do not.

Benn's Media Directory, Benn Business Information
Services Ltd, PO Box 20, Sovereign Way, Tonbridge, Kent
TN9 1RQ. Tel: 0732 362666. Lists over 15,000 UK organisations, publications and broadcasting stations. There are
also European and world editions. Available in many
large public libraries. £99 for a single edition.

Freelance Market News, Cumberland House, Lissadel
Street, Salford, Greater Manchester M6 6GG. Tel: 061–745
8850. For markets accepting freelance copy this monthly
publication is in a class on its own and well worth consulting.

Magazine News and **Magazine Handbook,** Periodical
Publishers Association, 15 Kingsway, London WC2B 6UN.
Tel: 071–379 6268. *Magazine News* is a bi-monthly trade
magazine about the PPA which has almost 200 members
between them publishing some 1500 titles. Their *Magazine
Handbook* (£50) is an annual statistical guide to the magazine industry and the two publications make fascinating,
if at times awesome, reading. Titles change hands frequently, merge with others and are relaunched under new
names. Buyers find themselves bought by bigger buyers,
individual magazines and even whole companies are
shifted in and out of publishers' portfolios and leading
editors or directors may defect or be lured to a former
rival's stable.

MDB Magazine Directory, The Magazine Business, 8
Tottenham Mews, London W1P 9PJ. Tel: 071–436 5211.
Fax: 071–436 5290. The vade-mecum of the newsagents'
trade. It lists over 3000 magazines that may be bought
from British newsagents – and is the only such directory
issued in full colour, making it attractive and easy to use.
In its pages you will find virtually all the information you
could want to know about any listed magazine: its cover
price, frequency of publication, circulation, the name of

the editor and other staff members, and the magazine's advertising rates. The last you may feel surplus to your needs but you will soon learn these figures can provide you with a helpful guide to the overall quality of any title and the timbre of what is printed on its pages.

To obtain a copy you could ask your friendly newsagent to bequeath you an old one he may be ready to throw away. This way you could gain a valuable idea as to what is available – or to what *was* available when it was published. It is updated and reissued twice yearly, in May and October. There is an accompanying smaller booklet that refers to just some of those in the larger booklet and all this is but a tip of the iceberg. Rather than rely on a copy you know to be out of date it would be wise to obtain a recent issue of your own.

Library magazines

Many public libraries keep a few magazines on display although those in small towns may not be able to do so. In my rural county it is a luxury we have learned to manage without, so I envy those of you with access to shelves of weekly and monthly magazines laid out for the eager browser by kindly librarians. Always check how your local authority organises its library service as the choice of whether titles will be on display or not varies from one place to another. If this service is available to you, do take advantage of studying whatever you can find – and perhaps even enjoy the convenience of sitting at a table to make your own notes. Visiting libraries further afield from your normal location may prove invaluable; those in county towns and main libraries in London boroughs often have excellent magazine displays and helpful librarians are generally ready to obtain back numbers on request.

I know several writers who have turned their original thoughts about what they were going to write upside down simply by becoming familiar with the magazines displayed in their local libraries. One told me he had grown quite fond of a particular title and felt sorry for it when an edition seemed unusually weak. Perhaps he will sell copy to it to help keep it afloat and follow that with an article to a writer's magazine about how to provide editors with life-saving material and help rescue a title from imminent closure.

Talking of writers' magazines reminds me of the two or three titles published specially for freelances. All include some listing of markets but not all the information given is accurate and much is out of date by the time it appears in print.

Something for nothing

The cover price of a magazine is generally split three ways: the retailer takes 25 per cent, 15 per cent goes to the wholesaler and the publisher takes the lion's share of 60 per cent. While the majority of magazines depend on their cover prices to boost advertising revenue it is surprising to find a few apparently freely given away. You can find them on aeroplanes, InterCity trains, outside Underground stations, in banks and building societies, estate agents' offices, supermarkets, hotel bedrooms and in numerous other places. Don't the publishers want the cover price?

Offering the public an apparent something-for-nothing is not as foolish as it might seem. Psychologically the readers (I almost wrote 'buyers' but of course there is no buying involved) are mentally pleased with the magazine before even opening it. The contents, regardless of what they might be, are greeted with positive acceptance because they are free; readers are not resentful at having wasted good money should an article fail to please, and if they approve of or delight in another they can bask in a self-satisfied glow of having got it for nothing.

From the publisher's point of view there are advantages to offset the obvious disadvantages of having no income from sales. Give away 10,000 copies of a magazine and you will have advertisers flocking to buy space in your pages. You can also aim at a carefully defined target readership more easily than can your larger paid-for rivals who (despite costly and intensive research) can't avoid missing the bull's-eye and wasting a proportion of their effort and money.

Magazines by post

A large number of periodicals are bought by prepaid subscription and delivered by the Post Office. Some subscription titles are also sold through the usual retail channels but others are available only (or mainly) by subscription, sometimes with enormous success. *Reader's Digest*, for instance, credited with being the highest-circulation periodical in the world, is sold almost entirely by prepaid subscription. More and more titles on visible sale in this country now also carry invitations to readers to 'take out a regular subscription', often coupled with the offer of tempting goodies. Readers might need sweetening at the prospect of paying for a twelve-month or 52-week period in one dollop instead of shelling out a less noticeable sum every now and then; and for the publisher, the money's in the bag with another reader secured for the year ahead.

Subscription selling is particularly successful before Christmas with inducements like 'Give her a present every month/week/etc.' Marketing managers will offer to send recipients special greetings cards or reward existing subscribers who recommend friends when the friends also become subscribers. Loyalty from readers for particular titles is highly valued by magazine publishers and winning readers by subscription is usually generously repaid: one editor may set up a 'Readers' Club' offering gifts and services, another could send out anniversary flowers and a third might organise coach outings or theatre trips for subscribers in particular areas.

Jack and Jill of all trades

Every industry, profession and occupation has its own trade press, i.e. one or more publications for people working in its own business. These periodicals will largely be about the business, whatever it is, and reflect the interests of its potential readers. They might be archaeologists reading *Current Archaeology*, grocers with *The Grocer*, enthusiasts of unidentified flying objects devoted to *UFO Times* or market traders scanning *World's Fair*. For our marketing purposes all trade magazines are grist to the mill and that includes such widely varying titles as *Motor Trader*, *Foundry Trade Journal*, *Manufacturing Clothier*, *Retail Jeweller*, *Poultry World*, *Dental Technician*, *PC User* and *The Banker*.

There are dozens of trade magazines and you may be surprised to hear a great many of them are happy to accept freelance contributions. The reason is not hard to find: behind the archaeologists, plumbers, car mechanics, market traders, musicians, *et al.* are people who do not just do a job of work.

They have other interests to occupy their spare time and at work or at play they (like everyone else) often like a touch of humour. Don't imagine trade magazines are solely devoted to 'business' matters; study of them will soon reveal this is not so.

You don't have to be a builder to sell to a magazine for builders any more than you have to be Jewish to write for a Jewish magazine or a computer expert to sell to the computer market. I am not a builder, Jewish or a computer expert but I have sold to all three types of periodical. I have also sold countless articles to the medical press over the years, all written from my viewpoint of being the only non-medical member of a large and otherwise entirely medical family. Yes, the background for this copy came naturally to me so it was (and is) a matter of 'writing about what you know'. But for some time I also wrote a light-hearted column for a publication read by engineers working in heating and ventilation about which I know nothing at all. In the latter case much of my copy centred round comical situations resulting from customers' lack of knowledge of the trade. I suspect my own genuine ignorance was more of a help than a hindrance in selling my work. Even knowing nothing can sometimes be useful!

In-house and little presses

Hundreds of companies publish in-house magazines for their staff and other interested people – from supermarkets to superstores, insurance companies to banks, travel companies to motor manufacturers. In all these, the general tone, as with those discussed in the preceding paragraph, is not that of the trade or business sponsoring the magazine but more for the 'ordinary' non-technical reader. Where do you find these in-house magazines, especially if you are not part of a business or company issuing one and do not know anyone who is?

You could ask for information about in-house publications, contacting the Department of Trade and Industry's company registry at Companies House or the British Library's Business Information Service which is the leading business library and also a public library. Details of both are to be found in Chapter 5. Enquiries may be made by telephone as well as in person although the latter is advised if possible. Perhaps the most practical way to find a personal opening is to talk to someone working in any capacity for a large organisation or company.

He (or she) will know of any in-house publication and, with luck, provide you with a few recent issues.

These magazines exist for two main purposes: to keep employees informed about what the company or organisation is doing and to strengthen unity and loyalty within it. For the observant freelance reading between the lines there are often opportunities for articles to inform, interest or entertain readers on topics quite apart from the organisation's mainstream occupation and frequently such opportunities are open to outsiders as well as company employees.

Around the country there are some 300 or more 'little presses' busy churning out magazines and seldom attracting much attention. Their publications are usually of individual attraction to particular groups of readers so circulation may be low and cost-effectiveness a monthly or weekly gamble. Some, the majority perhaps, keep going only by their readers' willingness to pay high cover prices, in effect subsidising the enterprise, and many get by on just a wing and a prayer. But despite their general non-viability (or perhaps *because* of it) they maintain a special place in writers' affections and the topics they cover vary enormously. To discover more you might like to contact:

The Association of Little Presses, 30 Greenhill, Hampstead High Street, London NW3 5UA.
Tel: 071–435 1889.

For future features

You open a consumer or trade magazine and find a large feature on, for instance, lawn care and garden fertilisers. Surrounding the columns filled with the article itself are advertisements for various gardening items. Of course these are carefully placed to catch the eyes of keen gardeners. Readers sufficiently interested in lawn care might be in need of a new mower, perhaps, and the latest in fertilisers could tempt many newcomers who hadn't heard about the benefits they could bring to the garden.

How did the advertisers know there was going to be an editorial splash about lawn care in that particular issue? And how did they buy advertising space on the most appropriate pages in the right edition of a particular magazine? Well, it certainly wasn't luck! Advertisers, like writers, must work to the vital lead time we've talked about elsewhere in this book: the lapse of time that it takes for a magazine to fix everything that will eventually be published in a particular issue. But even observing the lead time, how do they know what will be published in editions three, four, six or even eight months hence?

The answer is that they consult an editorial features directory which releases information about forthcoming editorial programmes, quotes dates by which copy must be received for particular editions and gives names, addresses and telephone numbers of editors or editorial contacts. These services are available to anyone, although they are not cheap. At first sight they might seem of little use to writers except to indicate what is already going to be covered. But – and this is where their real value lies – at the time of listing in an editorial features directory only a general editorial plan has been declared. The bones of topics to be covered have been exposed; most of the meat remains to be written . . .

Some services offer a try-out service for a short time at reduced cost and it is always worth finding out further details for yourself. One of the best to consult is:

Advance, Themetree Limited, 2 Prebendal Court, Oxford Road, Aylesbury, Bucks HP19 3EY. Tel: 0296 28585. This company provides a booklet every two months giving thousands of leads for future editorial work in consumer and trade magazines such as *Ideal Home, In Britain Magazine, Essex Life, Farmers Weekly, Nursing the Elderly* and *Charity*. For *Cat World*, for example, I see (reading the January *Advance*) that the April *Cat World* will feature cruelty-free products, welfare and charities, and cat treats. I also note the editorial contact is Joan Moore on 0273 462000 and the editorial copy date is six weeks prior to the cover date.

Sunshine and showers

The sun doesn't shine all the time even on the most optimistic and determined freelance. It would be folly to suggest everyone can write for every market; in fact it is a blessing this is not the case or the competition to sell to magazines would be vastly increased. Maybe you will occasionally make an initial choice of market only to discover on closer study that it is really not for you at all. This could be valid reasoning but be careful not to let too many potential markets fall away with this not-for-me excuse or you'll be throwing good babies out with the bathwater; making such decisions is not easy.

So despite my constant encouragement to work hard (for that is what sustained success demands) don't *always* assume you can crack any market, however tough, with sheer dogged perseverance. I have sometimes ignored my own common sense and arrogantly persisted with what was (I realised only later) an unsuitable approach or an unwanted theme. Perhaps it is only because I've wasted time, effort and had my pride dented that I now appreciate my own stupidity. In your excitement of discovering more markets than you ever thought existed and in your eagerness to write for as many of them as possible, keep a cool and controlled assessment of what you are doing or your work will suffer rather than flourish. There is a limit to our capabilities, even to those of the best writers among us.

4
Structure and style

What type of article are you planning to write? Identifying its purpose is the first decision to be made. Is it to instruct readers, to tell them something, to reflect on the past, to raise protest, to amuse, to appeal to deep feelings – or what? Editors want articles that do all these things and more. They want material of all types, but only, as we saw in the last chapter, what is relevant and timely to their magazines and policies.

When you read a published article, ask what the writer's purpose was in writing it. What is its appeal? We may assume the subject matter is what the editor knows readers wanted or it wouldn't appear in the magazine, but how is it written?

Identifying style and structure

Is the style jokey and friendly, informal enough to make you feel at ease but sufficiently well informed to give you no doubts about the value of what you are reading? Or perhaps the tone is commanding or distant, with a 'gap' between the writer and readers, i.e. written with the voice of unquestion-able, even severe, authority. What is best for one market is not necessarily ideal for another, of course; but how would you describe the article's style?

Above all, is it well constructed? Do the words and sentences sit comfortably on the page so you read it without any hesitation or misunderstanding? If you lose interest, find yourself looking back to check something in the paragraph you've just finished or realise you are skimming the whole piece quickly in the hope of spotting at least something worthwhile in it, it is the writer's fault not yours. The article, should you ever see such a one in a magazine, suffers from a faulty or non-existent structure. In this chapter we shall con-sider these vital ingredients of a publishable article: its mood, its structure and its style. We'll begin by pinpointing some of the most commonly published types of article.

Practical articles

If what you are writing is purely practical – giving information, perhaps – it must be logical, well ordered and do the job it sets out to do. Talk of 'style' is often superfluous as it virtually takes care of itself. A practical piece may give instructions or urge readers to some course of action. In such an article it is not hard to reach the readers. They are seeking what you are offering so you are half-way there when they settle down to read and follow your advice. This is where clear structure proves its worth. The essential ingredients are lucid organisation of information, sticking to the subject, establishing a logical sequence of points to make and adopting a style appropriate to the market. In short: contents, order and style.

Order is easy to arrange if you are instructing readers in how to build a wall, for instance, or ice a cake. Take the action in stages, dealing with each in turn and you can't fail. Although you may not write the words *first*, *next*, *then*, and so on, think of the sequence in such a way and you will be sure not to miss out any steps by mistake.

Factual writing

This type of article is written to inform readers and perhaps, when they've read it, influence them to change their minds on some important topic or at least reconsider what might have been hidebound or previously unchallenged assumptions or beliefs.

Such writing needs a good deal of prior preparation. You will be wanting to include plenty of facts, quote opinions voiced by other people in the field under discussion, record earlier points of view, put events and statements in historical perspective: all this takes time and hard work to prepare. Libraries may have to be visited, copious notes taken, interviews arranged and conducted. Background facts, possibly never to be included directly in the article itself, will be needed to support your argument or give credibility to whatever you are voicing for readers to consider. The article will be strengthened with telling anecdotes, irrefutable figures and quotations from well-known people, all of which need finding, recording and sorting before you can use them for the effect you want to achieve.

Make no mistake about it: factual articles are tricky, time-consuming and quick to trip you up if you don't get them right. The section on 'structuring' (later in this chapter) is essential reading before you begin.

Narrative articles

Narrative? Doesn't that mean telling a story – a fictional story? It does, but there is also scope for the narrative mode in writing articles. You may find the word 'feature' attached to this sort of article more than to others and some editors would refer to it as nothing else. In short, if you have a thumping good story to tell from the heart (and the market is suitable, of course) writing it in narrative form is often the best way.

A friend whose life I have watched closely for many years is one of this country's sufferers from a rare disease of the central nervous system. I'll call her Shirley although that isn't her real name. During one unbelievable week when she was in her mid-twenties, the disease hit Shirley with a devastation her family and friends found impossible to grasp. She was a bright, bubbly and athletic girl who was the leader of the tennis team in her first university year. Within days she changed almost beyond belief. She could not, and still cannot, move, talk, breathe unaided or even open her eyes. Able to do nothing at all for herself, she relies on the caring ministrations of other people and on an array of medical accoutrements for survival from one minute to the next. She can see if her eyelids are held open and, by some miracle, her hearing is unimpaired. Now in her forties, she knows her condition will never improve and there is no possibility of a cure.

But modern technology has come to her aid. With a formidable battery of the appropriate equipment she can write and even talk. For a long time I have been struck by her marvellous sense of humour. Shirley, imprisoned in a life many people would think not worth living, cheers other folk up when they are downhearted and makes *them* laugh. Forgive me if I talk about her too much but this, as many editors agreed, was a story that must be told. And there were many aspects of it . . .

What did those hideous days do to her young agile brain as they wrecked her body? How has she come to terms with her position since then? Does she seek an explanation? This aspect of the story, concentrating on her personal recollections, reactions and philosophy, interested most readers. It was published in two religious magazines and one of general interest with a penchant for uplifting copy gently reminding readers of their own health and good fortune. A sports title for students wanted a piece about how Shirley now teaches beginners tennis – yes, *teaches tennis* – and writes instruction manuals for them. More than a dozen magazines in several countries have published articles on a range of topics associated with her life. Some simply told her incredible story. Others aimed at helping those less severely handicapped and a few demonstrated how the practical aspects of caring for her could help other handicapped people.

Shirley reads (or is read) everything her family and friends can find published about her and doesn't automatically approve of it all. At times she can be grumpy, sad or impossible to please like the rest of us. But I and others know her so well we can spot when she is delighted with life, albeit she cannot display emotions as we can. She knows she is a very special celebrity and therefore someone to write about. But happy as she is as a subject, she refuses to write about herself. 'Self pity!' the words crackle out of her talking machine. 'You won't catch me going down that road.' What a girl, Shirley. What a story.

Nostalgia and reflection

Be careful writing articles of this type. They are satisfying to write as they usually involve talking about our personal affairs. What is more pleasant than a nostalgic return to once-loved places and faces, happy childhood memories evoking the delights and contentment of long ago? In truth, what may have been pleasures for us in the past and are winsome to recall now are almost certainly boring for other people.

That is not to say nostalgia doesn't have a valid place in a writer's armoury: it does. Just making sure you are writing for the readers and not for yourself will keep it in its proper place.

Specialised articles

Take any group of people interested in a special subject and write for them: such articles are what we might call 'specialised'. It doesn't matter what the subject is: politics, dancing, gardening, being parents, sport, pets, music, health – whatever the topic there will be a magazine about it and probably more than one.

The way to write such material is, of course, to study the relevant published magazines and talk to people. We all love talking about our hobbies and special interests and you'll have no difficulty finding folk to answer all the questions you can ask. (See Chapter 8.)

Business and trade stories also fall into this category. They often crop up as by-products in other mainstream articles. For instance, in the course of my interview with a city financier about his millionaire status he mentioned his humble start in a small factory in Rochdale. In those days he kept a little brick in his empty sandwich box. He told me he didn't want the other men lifting the box, noticing it was light and discovering it always was because he couldn't afford any food during the working day. This was laughed off during the interview itself but made a fine start to a piece about the man in a professional journal for businessmen, where the editor favoured rags-to-riches stories about the currently famous.

A large number of articles don't readily fit into any identifiable 'slot'. That is the beauty – and the challenge – of writing non-fiction: there is *nothing* you cannot write about, the world is your raw material and you are restricted only by your own ability.

Structuring

Although devoted to my own electronic writing equipment (and like many other writers almost convinced I couldn't now write anything without it) I find there is still little to beat a large sheet of paper and a stout pen when the first jumbled whiffs of an idea come into my head. Any piece of writing lacking a basic plan is far more likely to founder in the writing than one given at least a simple outline of what it's trying to say and how it's going to do it.

Making a structure plan before you start will keep your head clear as you write the piece. It helps you to see where you're going, guides your arguments in the best order and stops you wandering too far from the point. A plan is as valuable to many writers, particularly at the beginning of their careers, as is an architectural design to a builder or a knitting pattern to a knitter.

Before we can make a plan we have to recognise (which doesn't mean overemphasise) the ingredients of all writing.

We express what we mean using three groups of words: sentences, phrases and clauses. A basic understanding of how they differ from each other is not essential but may be helpful when we have to correct something that doesn't mean what we intended it to mean. A sentence contains at least one finite verb (i.e. a verb that has a subject it agrees with in person and number): *He walks in the park.* Phrases are groups of words which don't make sense on their own and have no finite verbs: We cook *in the kitchen.* Clauses cause the most trouble: they are sentences themselves and are used to join others into longer sentences: *When the children come* we will play in the garden *if it is fine.* The joiners are known as conjunctions. Words like *if, when, that* and *but* are commonly used conjunctions.

There is sound logic in the proposition that a sentence expresses one idea and a paragraph one aspect of the topic you are writing about. It is sensible because it works: articles built on this concept cause few problems to writer or reader. They are simple to understand and leave both with a feeling of satisfaction.

In this structuring method the opening sentence of each par introduces its special point which is expanded in the par's remaining sentences. (*Par* is journalist shorthand for *paragraph* and you'll find it often in these pages.) Clear paragraphing renders your article easy to follow as you deal with your points step by step.

Here is an explicit structure plan for a straightforward problem-solving, instructive or informative article:

Opening par – define the problem/task/topic
Par 2 – support with facts/figures/anecdotes, etc.
Par 3 – show how to solve/work at/gain from solution
Par 4 – substantiate with more examples/stories
Par 5 – wrap up with good results/spin-offs, etc.

To make a plan for your own article, marshal all your information and the points you want to present, be they at this stage on a single sheet of paper or in the form of random notes, jottings, cuttings and as yet unresearched headings. Collect everything where you can at least survey the whole range of what is likely to be your completed article.

Now choose your opening point (with care, as outlined below) and mark it to take its place on a clean sheet of paper under the words OPENING PAR. Then make a note of its intended length.

If any one part of an article is more important than all the rest it is the opening and not just the first paragraph or even the first sentence. For top place in the influential stakes the opening *few words* win every time. Attract the instant attention of editors – nay, rivet their attention – and they will read the rest of your copy in a receptive frame of mind. They know their readers' tastes (their jobs depend on such knowledge) and if you can please them at the beginning of your article you are off to a good start.

So a confident opening is crucial. It will set the tone and mood of the piece and provide immediate insight into the purpose of the article. Whether your subject is how to improve your swing in golf, the problems of population control in China, mending broken furniture or whatever it may be, the opening par *must* answer the primary question 'What's it about?'

However short you make it (I emphasise brevity because effective first pars pay dividends) the sentences should be positive and punchy or readers' eyes will wander in search of something more interesting. A short opening par gives the editor an instant indication of the article's value and needs less sub-editing when (not *if*, you note) it is accepted.

The market you have chosen will determine how you word the first par, sometimes referred to as the 'lead', and there are countless ways of writing it. Start with an anecdote? A shocking revelation? A quote from a famous person? Often you can't do better than state a simple fact:

American baseball star Hank Aron received more letters in one year than anyone has ever received before.

Perhaps you and your market prefer:

More than 900,000 letters fell on the mat last year.

Or:

Baseball sent wages soaring last year – for postmen.

As the leading par is so important we must be sure not to spoil it with rambling, shapeless or ill-planned paragraphs afterwards. While every good article begins with a strong opening, the order in which subsequent pars are arranged can make the difference between eventual success and failure.

When you read a professionally written article you will leave it with several distinct impressions in your mind: those impressions are there because the writer arranged the arguments and points in a particular order. This order lends weight to some important pars and allows others of less value space further on in the article. You, the reader, absorbed the result of clever paragraphing without even realising it existed: that is one proof of skilful structure planning. In the same way, arranging pars in relation to each other also needs key sentences inserted at the most meaningful points, drawing attention to important aspects of your theme where you wish to make them.

What supporting matter do you have (or can you find) to make sure readers are hooked? That will go in par 2 in the structure plan above as a promise that it will be worth reading what you have written.

Par 3 takes the argument further and here you would broaden your scope by bringing in a new line of reasoning or another slant on the topic. This in turn could be followed in par 4 by further substantiating anecdotes or facts to strengthen the points made in par 3.

You could continue the loop of pars 3 and 4 umpteen times, introducing more new aspects and more points-of-view to your story. But wait! A structured plan is only that: pursue it without variation and it may blight the whole work, turning it into a flat repetitive article written without much imagination or skill: a piece no editor will want because he knows no reader will be interested in reading it. 'Imagination and skill'? We shall have more to say about these later in this chapter.

Varying your method of sentence and paragraph construction not only makes the article easier to read but also presents a more pleasing layout on the page. Only last week I read an article submitted on spec to a magazine: seven of the first eight sentences and *all* six pars began with 'I . . . ' There are many ways of bringing individuality to the writing of sentences, indeed such variety often lends to words and phrases richer meaning than we can convey in stereotyped or overused methods in daily use. If you feel the need for further instruction I strongly recommend the following:

The Good English Guide, compiled and written by Godfrey Howard. Pan Macmillan Ltd, Cavaye Place, London SW10 9PG. Tel: 071–373 6070. Acclaimed as the 1990s replacement of Fowler, this is a guide to the use of English in which grammar and vocabulary are dealt with realistically, taking a consensus on where to draw the line over spelling, meaning and sentence structure. It's all designed with the user, i.e. the writer, in mind and adds understanding, sensitivity and pleasure to writing, offering countless new insights into the use of English. £16.99.

Notwithstanding the value of making a structured plan before starting to write, it is worth remembering that even the most carefully designed plan should not be adhered to *regardless of the cost*. The questions 'How many words should there be in a sentence?' and 'How long is a paragraph?' arise frequently in tutorial classes for beginners and there are no answers. I can only say, as with the opening pars we've been discussing above, err on the side of brevity if in doubt. If you have allotted or plan to allot a large number of words to a sentence or a great number of lines to pars, think again.

The same advice applies to the whole theme. Your subject matter and the way you are tackling it will dictate your structure but if you are new to this writing business I urge you not to make the whole article too long. Six or seven sentences in a par usually suffice but it 'ordipends' (that's a word I thought existed when I was a child: I was amazed to discover it didn't and still feel it should). It is easy to get carried away when writing about a topic you find interesting, the more so if you are using a modern word-processor. Such a machine is a great beguiler, letting thoughts flow out of our heads as fast as our fingers can flash over the keyboard. A friend newly trained in typing at speed complains he was never tempted to overwrite when he had to fumble for each key. So much for progress!

Linking words

Words linking pars should be unforced and lead the reader into accepting the new par's point without difficulty. These are often called 'joiners' and most serve more than the purpose of linking one par to the previous one. *And* carries on with the purport of the previous par, *for* introduces a reason, a result, or a new development while *so* usually means *and the consequence is*, or *was*. An alternative viewpoint may be introduced by *but* and *now* should be used with caution: too often it means *at last we're getting to the point*.

Change for change's sake is bound to be a jerky and artificial intrusion but vary the methods of linking one paragraph to another and your prose will flow smoothly. Be sure each joiner is appropriate to its task: to bring a new point to the reader's attention.

In the sample structure plan above I refer to setting a length for each par. As with the plan itself, don't necessarily stick to your preset length come rain and shine. Although *some* length has to be set in the plan to let you consider how much a par's point is worth to the whole theme, do not feel you must not depart from the plan on this matter. Sometimes as you write your article you may feel that, somehow, it is not balancing very well. Maybe a par should be shortened here or another lengthened a little there. That's perfectly all right; indeed it is an encouraging sign that your instinctive writing ability is taking over and giving you new confidence.

So forcing your work to abide by the structure plan you've made for it is a mistake: covering a point in a preset length and counting it done when you've written 50 words, say, is unnaturally jerky and rigid *if it doesn't feel right*. Strictures show in structures!

On the other hand the requirements of the market regarding the length of the overall article mean you cannot take all the time and space in the world to ramble on and round about in every sentence. Such diffuse and loose writing is certain to be unacceptable. Somewhere in the middle lies the best course: to write concisely and to the length required but with the article well shaped and each paragraph or point receiving its proper proportion of the total wordage.

How to end

If you have started with an anecdote, closing your piece with another, perhaps relating to the opening one, can give it a satisfying completeness. There are other ways of finishing off (remember a lingering farewell often kills otherwise acceptable copy) but however you do it, if you've given readers what your opening par indicated you would give them, you will have done a good job. No matter what your purpose was in writing the article, whether you've roused them to passion, soothed their fears and troubles, lulled them with fond memories or provided the solution to mending their leaky radiators, always aim to leave them contented.

Style

We've set up the framework, now what about the style? The skeleton needs clothing: back to market study we go.

Everything we need to know about a magazine's style is right there on the pages already published. What is known as 'house style' is dealt with later in this chapter but what we are studying here is the overall 'tone' of freelance material. What is it that distinguishes one piece of written work from another? That quality we so vaguely refer to as 'good': what does it really mean? The imagination and skill we referred to earlier are part of it.

To read an article or even a paragraph and be left with a glow of satisfaction is one of life's real pleasures. Most readers are happy to accept it and don't try to explain it. We writers must analyse it in some detail if we hope to encompass such easily flowing writing in our own work. I do not believe it always comes naturally even to those apparently most skilled although I am sure the art improves with constant practice. We also help ourselves, perhaps without realising it, by constant and widespread reading. There are many ways of improving style and, although their purpose is to make it look 'natural', their usage is, in fact, the very opposite. This is the art that conceals art; and the greatest concealment is the hiding of the tools we use and the artifices we resort to.

Stylistic tools

If you've read widely without being aware of what are termed 'figures of speech' you can be sure your reading matter has been well written. These are literary devices we writers employ to 'keep 'em reading'; they help us use words to make particular effects. Here are four of the most valuable:

Simile. Simile compares different objects by referring to what they have in common and is often preceded by *as* or *like*:

She sailed up in the air like Mary Poppins.

She sailed up in the air as Mary Poppins did.

Note the difference: *like* is followed by a noun but *as* comes before a clause (containing a verb).

Metaphor. This is writing in a figurative sense creating a picture image:

He hit the nail on the head.

It also compares two things without using *like* or *as*:

The plan was a dead duck.

Note: Simile says one thing is *like* another: metaphor says one thing *is* another.

Euphemism. Softening the impact of something hard for readers to accept is achieved by euphemism – clothing it in elaborate words:

I regret your services are no longer required. (You're sacked.)

Idiom. Every language has its own little quirks and oddities: this is idiom. Between themselves English speakers don't have to explain what they mean by *a fly in the ointment* or *she's the one who wears the trousers.* There are countless other idiomatic phrases that embroider our language and writers for magazines should not be frightened of using them. Wisely handled they can add richness and variety.

Rhythm

Have you thought of written work, typed words on sheets of paper, as having pulses and cadences? These determine the overall effect on the 'inner' eye and the pleasure (or otherwise) brought to the senses. Does what you've written have rhythm, albeit in words and not music? For there is undoubtedly a pleasing word rhythm and all the best writing, whatever its genre, has it.

It may be a question of unison. In the article's sections (its architectural divisions, as we discuss above under 'Structuring') is it one family? Does the introduction strike a chatty informal tone, is the middle formal or pompous? And what is the tone of the later parts or the end – neither formal nor chatty, but stilted or vague? Of course I have to exaggerate the problem to make my point plain: there should be, indeed there must be, *rapport* in the separate parts if the piece is to read as an harmonious whole. Lack of accord often makes readers feel uneasy: it's as if they realise something is amiss but can't quite put their fingers on what it is and a small bit of their trust and anticipation in what they are reading is lost.

An example: *I love skating and chocolate.* If compatibility is to be maintained the objects of the verb *love* should be constructed in the same way. In this case the first object of *love* is *skating* which is a noun (in technical terms a *gerund*) formed from the verb *to skate*. The second object of *love* is *chocolate*, another noun. Somehow the pairing of a gerund and a noun, unequal partners, brings the reader up with a jerk. You may have noticed how effective such writing can be when used deliberately perhaps for comic effect. In these cases the whole point is, of course, that it *does* sound odd and therefore will give us a laugh because it is not what we expect. But be wary of using it in ignorance. Stage pianists know you have to be able to play the piano well before you can play it *badly* well.

It is easy to correct errors in harmony and there are countless ways of skinning a cat, as my grandmother used to say; as a devoted ailurophile (off to the dictionary for you?) the sentence still makes me shudder.

Clarity

I have an obsession with clarity. But I do not apologise. If you, the reader of this book, gain nothing else from it but the conviction that clarity is the premier over-riding quality essential to all good writing, you will have learned the most valuable fact any writer can learn. If you can't write (or learn to write) so readers can understand what you've written, you will never succeed. Perhaps your structure is weak or your research has been inadequate. Do either 'show through'? That's a bad error but one difficult for us writers to spot, seeing it all subjectively. Maybe you've been talking in the wrong language, using words and phrases unsuitable for the readership. Misunderstanding has many causes. And it all adds up to lack of clarity.

I like the story of a public house in the West Midlands

called 'The Bird-in-Hand'. The landlord faced complaints about its new sign showing a curvaceous bikini-clad blonde. He explained he had simply asked the signwriter for a bird.

Tautology

The shortest way of saying what you want to say is often the best. Many words we use in speech are redundant, not necessary and would be better omitted. Those last few can go for a start. *Not necessary* and *would be better omitted* mean the same as *redundant*.

Phrases like *advanced forwards* and *reconsider again* don't need their hangers-on: advancing can only mean going forwards and anyone reconsidering anything is already considering it again. In formal speech tautology is evidence of poor construction (or perhaps a nervous delivery) and in casual conversation it is generally harmless for it has gone before we think it worth noting. In the written word it is inexcusable.

The *mot juste*

Not only must facts be accurate: words must be well chosen for their purpose. To each of us a particular word or group of words represents an image in our minds and we are only able to communicate with each other because, by and large, we share the same words for the same images. Communication depends on mutual understanding just as safe motoring depends (among other things) on drivers knowing what traffic lights mean and what road signs are telling us. But when we listen to someone talking in a language we don't understand, no 'image-transfer' takes place: we don't know the words used or what images they are trying to send us.

So all effort spent on fine phraseology, thoughtful structuring, earth-shattering revelations and the many aspects of article writing that take up our time are totally wasted if we do not use the 'right' words for the job. Only they will transfer the image you want passed from your head into that of your reader: the wrong words will move only part of the image or none of it. Worse still, they will create in your readers a concept quite different from the one you think you are giving them.

What if you need to use a particular word or a term but

cannot be sure your readers will understand its meaning? Tact is called for; you don't want to exasperate them by over-explanation nor annoy them by treating them as if they were half-witted. If you don't use the word or term in a context that itself makes the meaning clear, give a very short explanation in brackets directly after using it. Brevity and immediacy should avoid rousing readers' ire as they assume the explanation is for others less intelligent.

Fashionable words and phrases

In principle I support a popular campaign's aim to render every written or spoken piece as simple to understand as possible. But when it comes to a brisk and remorseless sacrifice of all words of more than one syllable in pursuit of that goal the campaign has lost me. Clarity undoubtedly begins at home but readers are not stupid. Although some may lack the educational achievements of others, even the least tutored in syntax and grammar will have become used to reading and understanding a wide variety of words. To reduce all writing to the starkest simplicity is as unnecessary as it is irksome. Our language is rich in words of every colour and degree and somewhere, if the writer can find it, is the word, the *only* word, for each occasion. Ah, you may be thinking, but what merit is there in the writer's finding it if the reader cannot understand it? Now we're back with our old friend: in this writing business most roads lead to market study, and here – again – we find the answer to how much we should or dare venture outside the market's published vocabulary. Once more common sense is the best guide.

Perhaps you love words as I do. I long to use old favourites and new ones as I discover them: fardels, pervicacious, gestalt, vulpine, telic, legerdemain, prurient, pellucid, cerulean, acroamatic, quotidien, tranche, pertuse, ukase, peirastic, jejune – there is endless bliss in a dictionary. A speaker on radio describes his burden as ineluctable, scholars seek recondite explanations and a Cumbrian farmer is philosophical about spending his life in ordure. I warm to them all for the words they choose.

And what about a new context giving old words an altogether fresh meaning? In *American Speech*, the journal of the American Dialect Society, I light upon *mall-jam* (to gather in a shopping mall for social reasons) and *bra* which is a drivers' nose-mask for protection 'from unfair readings that result in unjustified speeding tickets'. Perhaps these and other such gems will eventually cross the Atlantic and merge into common parlance here. Until they do I dare not use them in work for most UK magazines. It's not that we writers have to be mere followers of others in selecting the words we use; many so-called 'new' words and phrases were originally coined by journalists. But while untried ideas frequently command editorial approval, new words are more likely to court rejection and never be tested on the reading public.

Just occasionally we discover a word that seems to have moved the 'wrong' way in its development and here I am thinking of one virtually unacceptable on the printed page. But it doesn't deserve its present poor reputation as its past was an attempt to avoid giving the very offence it now causes. In seventeenth-century London Old Bailey clerks used many of their own home-made acronyms; one concerned prostitutes who were recorded as having been taken into custody *For Use of Carnal Knowledge*.

If the unfamiliar words a couple of paragraphs above sent you scurrying to a dictionary, can we rely on casual readers doing the same? Alas we cannot. Many magazines are sold on nothing more than the browse–like–buy impulse. Far from encouraging readers such etymological indulgence (see how difficult it is to stop once you start?) will drive them away at the gallop. We must forget our personal likes and dislikes, come down to earth and look at what the reader wants and will buy.

I have generally found it wise to stick pretty closely to what the language markets expect in my initial dealings with them, growing cautiously more venturesome as my reliability becomes established. Sometimes I've come unstuck at this point (growing too big-headed) and what I thought was a good market for me has decided I am not the writer it wanted after all. There could be many reasons for losing what I had hoped was a steady buyer of my copy: one of them might be that I'd strayed into using *my* choice of words in preference to *theirs*.

A final warning about words: be careful of trade names. So many have almost merged into daily language we hardly recognise them as such, but using them in a magazine article could cause problems. Hoovering the carpet, Sellotaping things together and playing with Lego may seem harmless occupations until advertisers of non-Hoover vacuum cleaners, non-Sellotape adhesives and non-Lego toys protest at the free plugs given to their rivals. No magazine can afford to invite such trouble and wise writers do not provide copy likely to start law suits.

Clichés

Clichés fall into the same potential pit: chiefly because of the old argument about their viability in 'good' writing. Moth-eaten ones are not hard to spot but often a phrase that seemed particularly appropriate at the time someone first used it (which is seldom the time we first noticed it) gains rapid popularity. Then brilliance dulls into tedium and the big family of hackneyed clichés welcomes another member. Should you avoid such words or groups of words? In determination to do so you can fall over backwards (an old one) and run the risk that studiously avoiding them will show through your work. If you suspect your vocabulary is not yet adequate to transforming the original brilliance of a cliché into your own words, an artificial avoidance of it may involve a tortuous trip round the houses (sic), leaving the very point you wish to make floundering without a supporting framework. Perhaps you never think in terms of clichés anyway, let alone other people's. Lucky you.

Be aware – and beware

'What is syntax?' repeated the schoolboy, giving himself time to think of an answer to his uncle's question. 'Syntax is putting words in order so they mean the same as the order you've put them in.' I wonder what Uncle said to that? At least the boy had the right basic idea. Syntax is the grammatical structure of individual sentences: the correlation of one word to another, one phrase to another and one clause to another. It is by no means as fearsome as it sounds and most of us speak and write all our lives using correct syntax without even being conscious of it.

So why bother with it now? Simply because an awareness of what it is and its importance will help us understand what is amiss when it breaks down. An offer from a local television shop came with this invitation:

As an existing customer I have a superb offer for you.

That doesn't make sense because *I* am the customer, not the shop. It is easy to write a sentence but what do you do when it doesn't say what you mean it to say? Sometimes it says quite the opposite. I recently saw the following published in a leading pet magazine as part of a reader's letter:

After suffering bladder trouble for some time the vet has recommended our dog has an operation.

I don't think we are expected to commiserate with the vet but that is exactly what the letter suggests. 'So what?' you may argue. 'We know it means the dog has been suffering, not the vet, so what is wrong with the sentence?' Of course we know what it means but that is not what it *says*. Dial 999 for syntax!

Since it's a matter of putting the words in the right order in relation to each other a simple dissection of the delinquent sentence will cure its ills, if not the dog. Copy its two halves out separately and consider where they should be to earn their keep. This is just one way to rearrange them (there are others equally effective) so there's no doubt about who was suffering and no hilarity raised by an unintentional howler:

When our dog had suffered bladder trouble for some time the vet recommended an operation.

Often putting the clauses and phrases in the wrong order causes confusion. Imagine you wrote:

Burglars broke into my house which was damaged by fire when I was away on holiday.

This could be understood as:

the fire occurred when the burglars broke in.

or

the fire occurred when I was away on holiday and burglars broke in on a later occasion.

The original sentence makes three statements:

[burglars broke into my house]
[which was badly damaged by fire]
[when I was away on holiday]

Change it to one of these to make your meaning clear:

Burglars who broke into my house when I was on holiday
set it on fire.
My house was damaged by fire when I was away on
holiday and then burglars broke into it.

Grammar and punctuation

Too many of us have memories of grammar we'd rather not
recall: school-days darkened by teachers trying to implant
what seemed inflexible and pointless rules into our heads.
Adverbs do this, prepositions must not do that, transitive
verbs behave differently from intransitive ones, something
agrees with or governs something else – oh, who wants or
needs to bother with grammar? Why don't we forget it and
get on with writing?

Despair not. Grammar is an essential part of language not
an immutable set of rules to be followed slavishly. Language
is changing all the time despite dyed-in-the-wool purists who
deplore the use of 'modern' words: and so it must. If it hadn't
developed over the centuries we should still be talking in
Anglo-Saxon or whatever tongue was in use when a nothing-
must-change law began.

No matter how good your command of grammar, spelling
and the use of special stylistic techniques, if you do not construct an article on a solid grammatical foundation you will not
make a success of it. It's such an important job there are even
computer software programs providing templates to make it
easier. One particularly for those with shaky grammar is:

Wordstar Correct Grammar, WordStar International
Limited, Chancery House, St Nicholas Way, Sutton, Surrey
SM1 1JB. Tel: 081–643 8866. Fax: 081–661 0070. Before
anyone throws this book down in horror let me mollify
purists by confessing I eyed this program with initial
doubts. Now, having investigated it thoroughly, I realise
they were born of ignorance. Everyone, even the most
articulate writer, can make foolish errors. In one quick
pass this program locates mistakes in grammar, punctua-

tion and readability. Yes, I've heard critics deplore attempts at an impersonal computer program trying to teach someone how to write but I am confident this will be a real help to those who need it. At dubious points in your text the program pauses and politely suggests how they may be corrected, giving you the option of ignoring any such suggestions, making alterations or rewriting your copy in your own way.

Correct Grammar has a further asset for writers keen to improve their knowledge of good grammar: at every pause for possible correction you can ask it *why* it has found fault and to explain the relevant grammatical rule. £49.

Another popular computer program proof reads your writing for mistakes in *style* as well as grammar. This is:

Grammatik 5, Reference Software International, 25 Bourne Court, Southend Road, Woodford Green, Essex IG8 8HD. Tel: 081–503 9933. Some types of writing require the writer to pay closer attention to grammar and style than others. This program guides you in many pre-defined styles as well as helping you customise your own. Is your current work technical, general, advertising, a report, journalistic, documentation – or what? In any of its styles *Grammatik 5* also differentiates between standard, formal and informal – so the choice is wide. £99.

Are you happy with full stops and exclamation marks? Is direct speech a danger area? In short, does your punctuation need a face-lift? It shouldn't be a problem if you remember its twin purposes are:

- to make your writing smooth and easy to read.
- to ensure what you have written is not misunderstood.

Like other subdivisions of grammar, faulty punctuation raises a wall between the writer and readers by making them pause and reconsider, frown, maybe try again – and probably turn to a new page of the magazine. The rules of grammar and punctuation are not carved in stone. They exist to facilitate communication *and for no other reason*. If you remain sceptical and fear I am going to lumber you with yet another set of instructions, amended from those you might have tried to learn years ago, delight in an acknowledgement that sometimes grammar isn't all it's cracked up to be and has to admit defeat. For example, the current lack of a both-sexes pronoun is a major shortcoming . . .

The gender problem

When wordsmiths decry the introduction of 'new' words to our language they might reflect how useful it would be to have a multi-gender pronoun. What a relief to put an end to the tedious business of she/he, his/her, etc. But no such unisex pronoun exists apart from 'one', a usage now outdated in common parlance and used only in deliberately formal or official mode. So what is the best way round the problem?

Changing from the singular to the plural often makes no difference to the context or sense of a sentence: let *a shop-keeper should always lock and bar his or her shop* become *shop-keepers should always lock and bar their shops.*

Consider removing excess words: *the infant will need treatment if he or she is to recover* may become *the infant will need treatment to recover.*

Sometimes a single word may replace a phrase: *the applicant wrote it by himself or herself* evades the gender problem as *the applicant wrote it unaided.*

House style

How do you write numbers and figures? Should it be 'Three blind mice' or '3 blind mice'? 'A boy of 6' or 'A boy of six'? Which is better – 'There are 31 days in May' or 'There are thirty-one days in May'?

Taking note of the house style of your intended market is part of market study itself. That means you will get to know a great deal about how the editor likes the magazine to look. You will know the favoured habits in punctuation, paragraphing, the use of capital letters and hyphens, writing numbers, dates, abbreviations and everything else that has to be set in type. Adhering to an established house style means, for example, that there is no uncertainty about whether to write 'Doctor Jones' or 'Dr. Jones' – with or without the point.

Keeping to the house style is not just a matter of placating an editor; inconsistencies not only irritate typesetters but also cause confusion. The purpose of house style is to ensure there is none.

Time was when house-style books were tossed around in every magazine and newspaper office. Nowadays with word-processors on virtually every desk the old books seem to have vanished. But don't imagine house style doesn't matter any more just because nobody can produce a style book. I know of at least two magazine offices where the word-processors in the features department have several aspects of house style built in. So staff writers cannot write *Dec 25th 1994*, for instance, when they should be writing *25 December 1994*. That's how important house style is.

Your chosen market's house style will be your best guide but there are a few general rules to observe in the absence of any others: spell out whole numbers up to twenty (four, seven, eighteen and so on) but use Arabic numerals for 21 and higher. It would be ridiculous, for example, to write 'the bill came to nineteen thousand four hundred and sixty-seven pounds and eighty-three pence'. Start sentences with 'Seven days make a week' rather than '7 days make a week' but in identifying a year '1993 began on a Friday' is always pre-ferred to 'Nineteen-ninety-three . . . ' Be careful about decades and spare the apostrophes: 'the 1920s were wild' is correct: the '1920's were wild' is not.

Royalty commands Roman figures (Henry VIII) as do some American offspring of tradition-building parents (Arnold Zimmer II) with the 'I' typed as a capital 'I' and not the number 1 or lower case 'l'.

As always the market is king. Watch its pages carefully for dates: May 8, May 8th, 8 May or 8th May? What about months? Nov or November, Feb or February, etc? And years: do they come before the month, before the day but after the month – or how? How does the magazine deal with fractions – half, ½ or .5? And what about 'per cent' or '%'? Taking the trouble to note these and other small points of usage and making your own copy observe the same rules will give the editor an instantly favourable impression that you have bothered to study the magazine. It will also endear you to the sub-editors who would otherwise have to amend the presen-tation of figures and numbers inconsistent with their normal practice.

Checking and editing

Before submitting your copy to an editor (or even presenting it to yourself in its final glorious print-out) go through it with an eagle's eye.

The ability to edit your own work is in many a professional journalist's opinion the secret of quality writing. It involves stepping outside your baby and viewing it dispassionately as someone (an editor) reading it for the first time. If that weren't difficult enough you then have to whip it into shape with a degree of cold purposefulness tantamount to self-flagellation. Excess wordage must be whittled away and some of your cherished phrases pulverised in your determination to prune and sharpen the article to its ideal balance within its word length. Oh my, it *is* hard and painful but it must be done. Perhaps if we remember we are partly doing it instinctively all the time it won't hurt so much. And it is a comfort to know the more writing we do the easier it becomes.

You could begin by making sure you are specific in what your article is saying. 'I've been to several countries in Europe but had never seen this . . . ' is more meaningful when you change it to 'France, Spain, Germany, Holland – but this was new to me . . . ' Scrutinise your adjectives, a common cause of flat predictable sentences, as it is easy to drift into the habit of assuming every noun needs a descriptive Siamese-twin. Adjectives should only earn a place on your page when they have something worthwhile to say, to add a meaning or an extra dimension that is valid at that point and cannot be said better in any other way. Spot the baddies, cut or replace them and their cousins, adjectival phrases, and then do the same with adverbs and their associated phrases, tidying up as you go. Sorry, all you *verys* and *reallys* and similar woolly-word intruders – out! And in thinking of *verys* it pays to be cautious about superlatives. Write that your neighbour's cat has the longest whiskers of any in England and you're asking for trouble. Somebody somewhere may produce a cat sporting longer whiskers. What is worse, your editor might no longer feel confident about other facts and figures you give him: if you were wrong once . . . Writing for magazines is a tough business.

Cut out anything not essential. Yes, I know that might mean abandoning some privately popular sentences and para-graphs but, if they exist only or mainly because they appeal to you, they could just be self-indulgent. Are you writing this only for yourself? If in doubt about the relevance of a particular piece picture yourself in the shoes of a typical reader. And remember an old maxim: if in doubt, cut it out.

Are you constantly editing your work? Perhaps you do it as you write it or in chunks at the end of a day's work or when you've completed the whole piece. Whatever your method, never feel you are frittering away your time. Re-writing (which is what editing your own work amounts to) is never dissipated effort. Most beginners don't do enough.

It frequently means the difference between rejection and acceptance.

5
Research

'What a waste.' A magazine editor pointed to a pile of unsolicited and unwanted copy on the floor by her desk. 'There were several good ideas in that lot but they had no depth. Their writers had made little or no effort to do any research. It's one of the most frequent reasons for rejection. Beginners either don't realise how vital it is to dig into the background of their stories, or they think they can get by with a brief skimming of the surface.'

So what *is* research? What did that editor mean – and many others say the same – in stressing the importance of it?

Briefly, it means getting your facts right. Thinking about it further, it means a good deal more: becoming an expert (temporarily) on your topic, being able to write with authority and confidence (which means knowing *more* than you are likely to reveal in your copy) and *never* having to gloss over tricky points because you don't know or can't be bothered to find the facts needed to support them.

If research sounds like hard work, take heart. It often proves surprisingly fascinating. A factual article without it will be too thin and weak for anyone to buy and a general article without corroborative facts and figures will lack the strength to stand up alone. Fortunately delving into facts magically infuses the writer with vigour; indeed, if *you* cannot work up enthusiasm as you are researching your topic, your readers (if you find any) are not likely to do so either. Do you remember, on the other hand, how you've sometimes read a piece so bursting with the writer's warmth you can almost feel it burning the page? I know several writers who become so addicted to research they discover it's hard to call a halt and get down to writing! Finding the facts may become an obsession: it's one you should cultivate rather than discourage. But it's also important to know when to stop. Getting the balance right is not always easy.

Ear ear . . .

A colleague once found himself in trouble because he did not think to ask anyone about the placing of a barn owl's ears. His article about these likeable enigmatic birds was a fascinating mine of information: the many different subspecies, where they live, the food they eat, their breeding habits, how to look out for them and so on. It was published in a family magazine and he knew the editor was particularly interested in wildlife. Being an accomplished artist my friend also sent several line-drawings. One published beside the copy identified the owl's facial characteristics – including its ears. When the article appeared there were complaints from owl experts; it seems a barn owl's ears are not placed symmetrically on either side of its head as one might suppose. In fact one ear is high up and about level with where the owl's forehead might be (if it isn't a solecism to so describe part of its face) and the other is further down almost level with the nose – er, beak. Very inconsiderate of the owl in the circumstances. I am using this as an example of how easily you can go wrong with factual matters. As my colleague ruefully discovered, it is essential to get the facts correct and to use the appropriate jargon what-ever you are writing about.

Finding the wood for the trees

In practical terms you have to decide what facts will be needed for your forthcoming article and what may also be useful information to hold on the side. While finding both these you must also avoid getting side-tracked. Keeping careful records of all your research material as you progress is the easiest way to juggle with these two occasionally contra-dictory aims.

I generally start with three categories of data held in sepa-rate files:

- Facts I know I will need.
- Any 'surrounding' data I may or may not use.
- Leads to further research, i.e. references found in source data for more detailed later research on the topic or on others suggested by it.

In all three files, with every fact or piece of useful information, I keep note of where I found it and when. This is crucial because a fact without such a note is a potential source of trouble and I simply dare not use it. If at any time I look through old files of research data and find something without a where-and-when note I throw it away in my own best interests. If it's sad to discard unreliable data it is also a pleasure to find newly discovered leads giving you ideas for other work in the future. This happens all the time and often I find the three files I started with grow to four or five or six . . .

In the files go cuttings, bits and bobs, promisingly useful or helpful titbits I come across in newspapers, magazines or anywhere else. I have a personal method of data security you might like to follow: when filing a sliver of information I haven't yet had time to check, I mark it with a big red question mark on the back. Turning over some research cuttings today, for example, for an article I am writing for an investment magazine, I find one with a red question mark on the back. It says 'A cheque for £187 million was the largest ever written in the history of banking.' Well, was it? I can't be certain – yet.

That is one of the joys of research: being able to find out. Somewhere, someone has the information you want. It comes in a variety of forms.

Reference sources

In this chapter we shall be discussing some of the most useful reference material for writers. As your needs will not be identical to mine (or anyone else's) when it comes to the specialist topics you are writing about, I will begin by listing some of the nigh essentials that benefit us all, regardless of what we write. There are several guides I could hardly manage without and the first book topping the list is every writer's treasure-chest on *how* to set about research:

Research for Writers by Ann Hoffmann, A. & C. Black, 35 Bedford Row, London WC1R 4JH. Tel: 071–242 0946. An invaluable handbook firmly established as an indispensable research guide offering a wealth of sound advice and solid information for every serious writer. The latest edition has been revised and expanded and now provides up-to-date information vital to the researcher. Contents include factual and historical research, organisation and method, where to find what you are looking for, family and local history, genealogy, picture research, information from and about overseas countries – and much more. £10.99.

Whitaker's Almanack, J. Whitaker & Sons Ltd, 12 Dyott Street, London WC1A 1DF. Tel: 071–836 6381.
Irreplaceable for anyone who regularly needs and uses accurate up-to-date information, this invaluable book offers a wealth of statistical, historical and current data on the UK and the rest of the world. Among other subjects it covers national and local government, the judicial system, foreign governments, capitals and currencies, finance, the arts, science, the media, education, sport, awards, honours and prizes. *Whitaker's* began as a journalist's scrapbook back in 1868 and has grown into the ultimate single-volume reference source on the market today. Easy to use, clearly and logically laid out, it remains unsurpassed in detail and accuracy. Standard £25. Concise £9.95.

Guinness UK Data Book, Guinness Publishing, 33 London Road, Enfield, Middlesex EN2 6DJ. Tel: 081–367 4567. A unique hard-back compendium of essential and inessential but fascinating information which includes up-to-date statistics, analyses and overviews of all aspects of British life. Among topics covered are social trends, the arts, central and local government, politics, the economy, defence, transport, science and technology, international relations, physical geography, major towns and cities, law and law enforcement, education, religion, the media and sport. Illustrated in full colour with maps, charts and diagrams, this book provides an easily accessible but comprehensive guide to Britain in the 1990s. £9.99.

The Media Guide, Fourth Estate Ltd, 289 Westbourne Grove, London W11 2QA. Tel: 071–727 8933/243 1382.
You're writing your piece and need important information – important *accurate* information. *The Media Guide*, a Guardian book, bulges with useful addresses and leads. Among them are contacts for the police, trade unions, sport, the courts and legal affairs, central and local government, hospitals, consumer watchdogs, prisons, travel, education, the fire brigade and pressure groups engaged in activities of all sorts. This handy guide covers all sectors of the media including magazines, newspapers, television,

radio, satellite, cable, news agencies, picture libraries, media bodies, media books and film/audio-visual libraries. The extensive contacts and research section lists key phone numbers (but few addresses) of government departments down to local council level. £9.99.

Electronic research

Writers need to research potential markets to write for and an unlimited number of topics or themes to write about. Both categories of research largely depend on reference books but the use of source material in electronic format is rapidly increasing and cannot be ignored. In non-technical language, for those new to the world of computers, it simply means joining your telephone to your computer with special but not expensive equipment so that when you call particular research services for help the information they provide appears on the screen in front of you. You can then save it on disk, print it on paper and do whatever you like with it. The service is generally paid for in one of two ways: by becoming a subscriber and receiving unlimited access to your source while your subscription remains valid, or by paying for individual calls as with the normal telephone system. You could use an 'on-line' service, as they are called, devoted to gardening, for instance, and call it up as often as you wished, or you could pay for one or two calls individually without being a subscriber.

On-line research is not complicated. It offers huge amounts of information without moving from your desk. You can tap into news, general information, stock-market prices, sport, train timetables and literally thousands of other topics; every day more are being added to the pool. But beware! Its attractions may pall when your telephone bill arrives. There are economies to be made by 'down-loading' (getting the information) straight into your computer at cheap telephone rates during the night, for all this wizardry can occur without your even being present, once you know how to set it up. The best advice I can offer on the problem of cost is to try it and see.

Even without joining the on-line world computer users greatly benefit from electronic research. It is not only quick and simple but also offers huge quantities of data in very small packages: the entire Bible, for instance, is easily stored on two or three low-resolution floppy disks available to the most basic computer-user. Another technique involves a format known as CD-ROM (compact disks with read-only-memory). These hold vast amounts of reference data and, although they only work with a special disk drive, more writers are realising that the cost of instant, accurate and almost unbelievably wide-ranging source material is quickly defrayed when compared with the time and money spent in traditional research methods away from one's desk. One compact disk can hold over 600 Mb of data compared to less than 1 Mb on an ordinary double-density floppy disk. The disadvantages that CDs are (at the moment) used only for storing information and cannot be added to doesn't stop their being a potentially revolutionary research tool. There is no doubt the use of CD-ROMs makes light work of consulting any works of reference that would take up walls or even *rooms* of shelf space.

Something for everyone

As I write this, a leading politician has made a fool of himself for making a bold public statement. It's not his view on the matter – itself so unimportant nobody will even recall what it was in a week's time – that has landed him in trouble, but his clear enumeration of statistics he claimed to be 'facts'. They weren't facts at all and his discomfiture was all the greater when they were quickly and easily checked. The quoted figures were not even *almost* correct, which might have been just tolerable coming from the mouth of a politician: they were wildly and hopelessly wrong. Who is going to believe this man's claims in future? At least he is only a politician; writers cannot afford to be so careless.

Now we're close to the end of the twentieth century any encyclopaedia covering it will be large. The following takes up more space on my shelves than any other single book, even beating my 1909 Dictionary of the Bible, and is more of an experience than a book:

Chronicle of the 20th Century, (Longman) Chronicle Communications, Chronicle House, 16 Invincible Road, Farnborough, Hants GU14 7QU. Tel: 0252 378000.
Specially prepared for Britain and Ireland, this takes a distinctly British perspective on a century that began in Queen Victoria's last years. Even in a tome this size the compilers have had to be selective but the format of a

page or two per month covers an impressive range. At
random I find, for instance, in February 1919 thirty-one
items ranging from UK boxing champion Bombardier
Wells being defeated to US President Wilson addressing
the Paris Peace Conference and the spraying of disinfec-
tant on London buses to prevent the spread of a flu
epidemic. Forward cross-referencing is simple although
there is no backward method, rendering the complicated
index essential. With colour and monotone illustrations.
£39.95.

The spectacular Chronicle range brings history to
life and includes many other reference titles covering
individual years since 1988: the Royal family, the French
Revolution, the Second World War, Aviation, Britain,
America, Canada and even the World. Together they
make valuable research tools.

Getting the facts correct is the essence of credibility and very
often amassing facts on which to build your article starts with
consulting a reputable encyclopaedia. This one adds the pleasure of colour and clear non-technical language to more than
1000 pages of world events, history, arts and sciences:

The Hutchinson Concise Encyclopedia, Century
Hutchinson Ltd, 20 Vauxhall Bridge Road, London SW1V
2SA. Tel: 071–973 9680. With tables and charts, illustrations and maps, many in full colour, this superb volume is
an indispensable guide to the modern world. Among its
17,500 entries you will find new nations, financial terms,
sporting greats, the human body, wildlife habitats, sports
and how they are played, the latest scientific and technical
terms – and much more. £15.95.

An electronic version comes from the same stable:

WordStar/Hutchinson Concise Encyclopedia, WordStar
International Limited, Chancery House, St Nicholas Way,
Sutton, Surrey SM1 1JB. Tel: 081–643 8866. Fax: 081–661
0070. The sometimes tedious job of scanning an index to
find what you want is done almost instantly by your
machine. As you type the first few letters the right location appears on your screen. Add another character or
two and the entry you want will be highlighted. Now the
full power of an electronic encyclopaedia is revealed:

select any word that takes your eye as you scan what is on your screen and you are immediately presented with the entry for the new subject, if there is one. Such a cross-reference system is the main advantage over the traditional printed book but it is not the only benefit. Others include the ability to browse in both directions through entries in indexed order, recalling a list of the entries already viewed and returning directly to any of them and then immediately back to the previous entry, no matter where it was in the index. The pack for DOS users consists of five 3½" 720K and/or three 5¼" 1.2MB disks plus a short but entirely effective manual aptly named 'Facts at your fingertips'. £49.

Eric Partridge (who died in 1979) was the leading collector of slang and he established the publication of reference books on the subject. Today the following is an invaluable research tool:

The Oxford Dictionary of Modern Slang, edited by John Ayto and John Simpson, Oxford University Press, Walton Street, Oxford OX2 6DP. Tel: 0865 56767. They call it 'slang with its sleeves rolled up' and a fair definition it is. An absorbing volume that includes more than 5000 twentieth-century slang words at their best and worst. Often hilarious and always fascinating. £13.95.

*Mis*quoting is a quick path to trouble and just one mistake can involve you in irksome and unwelcome correspondence. 'Only man needs to blush'. Animals don't.' Is this an accurate quote? And who said it?[1] The following are recommended:

The Concise Oxford Dictionary of Quotations. £4.95.
The Concise Oxford Dictionary of Proverbs. £3.95.

A simple-to-use disk program also provides an instant library of quotations:

WordStar Correct Quotes, WordStar International Limited, Chancery House, St Nicholas Way, Sutton, Surrey SM1 1JB. Tel: 081–643 8866. Fax: 081–661 0070. Access to more than 5000 quotes of wide variety from

[1] No: the correct quotation is:
'Man is the only animal that blushes. Or needs to.' (Mark Twain)

the contemporary, literary and historical on more than 600 topics. Search and paste into your own work from some 1500 sources, plus the means of adding your own quotes to the store. Easy and fast to use. Quotations are arranged alphabetically by topic with an 'author' list, cross references and a powerful search feature. For Windows applications and most word-processors. £49.

Chambers Dates, Chambers, 43 Annandale Street, Edinburgh EH7 4AZ. Tel: 031–557 4571. Lists more than 6000 important dates. (No longer in print but well worth finding.) .

British Humanities Index, The Library Association, 7 Ridgmount Street, London WC1E 7AE. Tel: 071–636 7543. An index of newspaper and periodical articles listed in subject order. Invaluable for finding references to material on obscure topics. Published quarterly and in annual volumes.

Government and official sources

PROs (public relations officers) and contacts from government, business, industry, education, trade, institutions, leisure organisations and the like welcome good publicity and are glad to help with queries:

The European Parliament UK Office, 2 Queen Anne's Gate, London SW1 9AA. Tel: 071–222 0411. Fax: 071–222 2713. Among all the arguments and in the face of so much rumour it is important to get the facts right. This is where to discover all you want to know about the European Union and its 344 *million* population.

Directory of British Associations, CBD Research Ltd, Chancery House, 15 Wickham Road, Beckenham, Kent BR3 2JS. Tel: 081–650 7745. Some 4000 different headings, subdivided into all you ever wanted to know about your subject plus a great deal more you never dreamed existed. Its abbreviations index alone is a lesson to all writers not to assume readers know what abbreviations stand for. Turn DBA's pages and the indices point you to a huge quantity of compressed information, so much that you'll find it hard to stop researching once you begin.

National Readership Surveys Ltd, 11–15 Betterton Street, Covent Garden, London WC2H 9BP. Tel: 071–379 0344. The leading organisation for measuring the readership of major newspapers and magazines. Publishes the National Readership Survey. Formed in 1992 after replacing JICNARS (Joint Industry Committee for National Readership Surveys).

Press Complaints Commission, 1 Salisbury Square, London EC4Y 8AE. Tel: 071–353 1248. Fax: 071–353 8355. A self-regulatory body for newspapers and periodicals, investigating complaints about editorial content. Replaced the Press Council and has no official powers of enforcement.

Libraries

Library catalogues exist for you to use as well as for the librarian. Many libraries now have them on *microfiche* and, if you are new to using the equipment, don't be shy in asking for help. Subject indexes lead you to classification numbers for the information you need and may also guide you along allied routes you'll find helpful. Librarians are trained and experienced in replying to your questions and you can save them and yourself time by being prepared. Be as precise as possible and explain why you want to know something if it helps in the search for it; a good librarian may suggest avenues of research that have not occurred to you. Remember, too, that many larger libraries, especially in major towns and cities, stock back copies of magazines and will let you borrow them for market study.

It is sad that the number of libraries open in Britain continues to decline and many of those that survive serve the public for fewer hours per week. Although the waiting lists for book borrowings are longer than ever, reduced budgets mean fewer books can be bought – lengthening the lists yet further. Sad too is the incidence of book-theft from public libraries; in their first national study of the problem the Home Office found that 4 per cent of the country's 220 million library books are lost every year, with unreturned books accounting for a third of the losses. Most standard reference books may only be consulted on library premises and may not be taken away, but despite this more non-fiction than fiction is borrowed. Due to sheer shortage of space, let alone money, not every library can stock every book you want to consult, but help is at hand in the shape of the Inter-Library Loan Scheme which enables branch libraries to obtain virtually any book. You may have to pay a small charge (although in some places it is still free) and you will certainly have to be patient as a wait of at least two weeks is normal. The rarer the book you want, or the more distant its location, the longer you could wait for it to be delivered to your local library.

Asking for the information you want is one thing, but what do you do if you don't know or are not sure of the title of the book you are looking for? A general survey of your topic can be invaluable. Ask your librarian if the library stocks the *Aslib Directory of Information Sources in the UK*. The seventh edition of this volume costs £250 and tables almost 7000 sources of information, listing organisations which charge for supplying information as well as those ready to issue it for nothing. The directory will reveal names and addresses of libraries holding their own information, most of which will be available for you to peruse. Then it is a matter of contacting the secretary or named person appointed by your chosen organisation to confirm when, where and how their records may be consulted.

Seeking information about business I've also found the following useful:

The City Business Library, 1 Brewers Hall Garden, London EC2V 5BX. Tel: 071–638 8215. Run by the Corporation of London.

The British Library's Business Information Service, 25 Southampton Buildings, London WC2A 1AW. Tel: 071–323 7454 (free) or 7457 (priced enquiry service). London's other main business library.

Companies House, Crown Way, Cardiff CF4 3UZ. Tel: 0222 388588. The home of the official registry of the Department of Trade and Industry. The registry is divided into parts covering geographical regions and the number for press enquiries is 0222 380062.

Leading magazines and newspapers have their own libraries and may be amenable to writers making genuine enquiries, particularly if prior written requests have been made.

The most comprehensive library of newspapers is:

The British Library Newspaper Library, Colindale
Avenue, London NW9 5HE. Tel: 071–323 7353. (From
1996: close to St Pancras Station.) This is the largest
library of its kind in the world. Take some form of identification along to gain access. Researchers are normally
expected to attend or to send someone on their behalf.
Assistants are very helpful with requests.

Words

The question of which words to use often falls into the
research field. Include 'egghead' in direct speech when writing about events in the 1940s, for instance, and someone will
take you to task. The word was unknown as a derogatory
term for an intellectual until 1953. For a fascinating investigation into 'yuppie', 'bobbysox', 'microwave', 'sit-in', 'bottom
line', 'flashback', 'jet set' and countless more neologisms see:

**Fifty Years Among the New Words: A Dictionary of
Neologisms 1941–1991,** Cambridge University Press, The
Edinburgh Building, Shaftesbury Road, Cambridge CB2
2RU. Tel: 0223 312393. Source material from the journals
of the American Dialect Society forms the basis of this
stylish hardback but British as well as American sources
have been consulted. Appealing to all interested in the
development of language and the introduction of new
words, intriguing sections explain how words came to be
formed and changed (by phonetic elision, blending, shift
of meaning) among other absorbing information. Editor
John Algeo describes the patterns of new words and
discusses some of the reasons for devising more. £35.

It is said that at least 100 people are looking up the spelling
or meaning of a word every second of every day. When you're
a writer you need the best reference material and here I list
several excellent dictionaries and thesauri (thesauruses is
given in most as a perfectly acceptable alternative plural):

The Chambers Dictionary. This is the new (and re-titled)
revised and updated version, surely holding the richest
range of English words, from Chaucer to the present day,
ever found in one volume. It is unrivalled in its coverage
of today's new words and meanings, including terms
from science and computing, commerce and marketing,

politics and the environment. Clearly presented with words simple to find and definitions easy to understand. Over 215,000 references and 300,000 definitions. A direct descendant of the renowned *Chambers Twentieth Century Dictionary*, now ready to take us into the twenty-first century. £22.50. For computer users both CD-ROM and floppy-disk formats are also available.

Concise Oxford Dictionary. The eighth edition has over 20,000 new entries and is as up to date in content and presentation as it is possible to be. It has been completely redesigned for greater ease of use and the definitions have been rewritten in straightforward everyday English. £12.95.

Collins Concise Dictionary Plus. More than just a dictionary, the 'Plus' includes some 15,000 encyclopaedic entries set alphabetically in the text. Twenty or more supplements cover the animal kingdom, the British monarchy, consumer durables, causes of death in Britain, countries and their leaders, among other topics. An excellent reference tool obviating the need to consult a separate encyclopaedia at every turn. £8.95.

Collins Dictionary and Thesaurus. A double volume arranged so that definitions, spelling, pronunciation, usage and a wide range of alternative words are instantly available without the need to consult a second volume or indeed to search in other parts of the same volume. £13.95.

Now regarded as virtually essential by many writers is the computerised version of the above:

Collins Electronic Dictionary and Thesaurus, Reference Software International, 25 Bourne Court, Southend Road, Woodford Green, Essex IG8 8HD. Tel: 081–503 9933. This is a single package for use on both DOS and Windows platforms. With it you're just a finger-press away from the definitions of 190,000 words connected to 275,000 synonyms, all fully updated. This must be the fastest, easiest and most comprehensive way of finding the word you want exactly when you want it. £90–£100.

Chambers Thesaurus. This paperback word-finder helps the writer struggling to find a forgotten *mot juste*. I find its special value lies in giving a list of possible words that have more (or less) of a particular ingredient, are more (or less) formal, are more (or less) euphonious; that, in short, have more (or less) of the elusive timbre I'm seeking. £6.95.

An amusing story came my way the other day about the accepted infallibility of a good dictionary. A schoolboy was called to account by a teacher for using the words 'by magic' in written work. 'Nothing happens by magic', she said, 'because magic doesn't exist.' The boy was genuinely surprised. 'But Miss', he replied, eyes wide, 'how can it be in the dictionary if it doesn't exist?' Her reply is not recorded.

And more . . .

Where do I stop in a listing of recommended reference books? Those that continue to prove immensely useful to me fill a lot of space in my study. I must mention three or four because I would feel as if I were betraying old – and new – friends if I didn't:

The Good English Guide, compiled and written by Godfrey Howard – see Chapter 4.

The Reverse Dictionary, The Reader's Digest Association, Reader's Digest House, 61 Curzon Street, London W1Y 7PE. Tel: 071-629 8144. You know what you want to say and that the precise word exists for you to say it – but when you reach for it, it's not there. Psychologists compare the situation to being on the brink of a sneeze. This invaluable book is a linguistic snuffbox and the relief it affords is considerable. It takes you from a familiar word connected with the idea to the elusive word you are looking for – from the word you know to the word you need. *The Reverse Dictionary* is also a fascinating vocabulary-builder. Rummage among its pages to enjoy some of the coruscating jewels of the English vocabulary – and happy *sternutation*. £19.95.

The Complete Wordfinder, The Reader's Digest Association. This is a gem of a book – and a large gem, weighing over 2kg. It is more than a unique and powerful combination of dictionary and thesaurus; its extensive contents include the history of English, terms for groups

of animals, etc., names for collectors (do you know what a
paroemiographer[2] does? No, I didn't but I do now), music,
electronics, languages, books of the Bible, proverbs,
geology, sports and games, alphabets, architecture – and
much more. Many appendices have line illustrations. A
reference book to read for pleasure as well as to consult
for research. £24.95.

Copy with care

It's remarkably easy to drop a nought or two from the end of
large numbers, easy and calamitous. So be precise when you
copy them from reference books and count those noughts as
carefully as any millionaire must. Likewise be scrupulous
with the names, addresses, telephone numbers and the
marital status of anyone you will be contacting for further
reference or writing about. I particularly mention this because
people are understandably fussy about their own personal
details. Get them right and you will improve your chances of,
say, gaining interviews. And when your article appears
carrying the names and titles of high and low there will be no
mistakes and nobody will be cross with you.

Serendipity

Happiness is surely finding the very book you want on your
own doorstep when you aren't even looking for it. Are you a
car-boot-sale addict? A jumble-sale frequenter? A charity-
shop casual? A school-fete family? I've picked up just what I
wanted in all these places. Often what I found wasn't on my
prepared list of 'books I badly need or must have' but proved
to be a useful addition to it, leading me into new and profitable avenues of research that hadn't previously occurred to
me. Many and wonderful are the bargains I've found at
such events; they are excellent value in the money sense and
have often proved *invaluable* in their use to me. Do you, like
me, avidly pore over piles of books friends or neighbours
might throw out when they spring-clean or move house?
Never miss an opportunity to add to your store of books for
research!

---

[2] A *paroemiographer* writes or collects proverbs.

6
Cast your net wide

An editor I once worked for referred to a small band of his most useful writers as IDAs. This stood for 'I'll Do Anything' and you can be sure the IDAs were always popular. They also enjoyed a richer and more varied writing life than many of those doing the same type of job for successive editions – and they were well rewarded for their versatility. Are you an IDA? This chapter delves into many ways of broadening your experience by writing more than just articles. What else do you turn to in a magazine's pages? What are those unusual or intriguing bits readers so enjoy? Who writes or compiles them? An IDA? *You*?

Making your own corner

Some of the topics in this chapter refer to pieces published regularly in magazines. A crossword, a chess column, word puzzles, nature notes, competitions, book reviews; establish yourself as a contributor of such copy and the editor is likely to offer you a regular spot in the magazine. 'Village corner', 'This month's bird', 'Famous railway engines', 'Notable men of the county' – the opportunities are bounded only by your imagination.

Whatever your idea, try writing half a dozen sample pieces for your eyes only before approaching an editor. There are several important questions to answer in private and 'Will I run out of ideas for my corner?' is only one of them. Before agreeing to a weekly, fortnightly, monthly or even quarterly commitment ask yourself if you can keep to a deadline. Think carefully about your answer. For many years I have been a regular contributor of specialised copy to a variety of publications and I know from dire personal experience that Heaven must almost fall before non-delivery or even lateness of copy can be excused. A friend came to stay? You've been too busy? Your typewriter or word-processor broke down? So what? The rest of the world still goes about its business and magazines cannot afford to wait for you. But take heart: editors, tough as they have to be to keep their periodicals afloat, are not entirely soulless. If you are *really* ill or face some dire crisis and you cannot keep to a deadline, let the editor know as soon as possible and he will see someone else does the work instead. Just don't let this happen too often or strain his forbearance too far!

Children's pages

Women writers have almost total monopoly of magazine pages published specially for children (I have to qualify that statement as I know of several men who do the job). When I was a young mother with small children I regularly read *Mother & Baby*, a parents' magazine. At the time it contained nothing specially aimed at pleasing the children of readers. If children had a part of this magazine, I mused, with pictures to colour and puzzles to work out, they would urge their mothers to buy it in preference to others of a similar type. I set to work.

With the invaluable help of an artist friend I produced enough copy and artwork for six consecutive issues. Then I wrote to the editor suggesting my planned column might suit her. I had 'softened her up' by contributing plenty of copy to her pages in earlier months, and had (of course) always been quick to alter or amend anything at her request. Would she now give me a regular page for children? Yes, she would.

The job was better than I had dared to hope: would I, asked the editor, take a whole page every month with occasional spreads of two or three pages several times a year, to give the children a real part of the magazine? The page began as a club for children to join. They received colourful badges which I bought for them from a leading manufacturer, and were offered a variety of competitions carefully designed for them. When I invited young readers to contact me the response was so great my small local sub-post office had to recruit extra sorters. Children wrote from all over this country and even from abroad. Success made me work very hard and involved a lot of activity, from meeting toy manufacturers (who supplied me with competition prizes) and companies producing babywear to interviewing groups of young mothers and infant teachers at play groups and arranging special treats for readers on selected occasions.

The job continued through three editorial changes and the stimulus of holding down a lively regular job did me good. Many tasks I undertook taught me more about magazine production and I was able to spread my net wider still. So whatever type of column you would like to secure, it is only sensible to set about getting it in a methodical and professional manner.

There are few things more satisfying than having your own corner/column/page published regularly. Your name and work get known as a specialist contributing editor, which helps you sell work to other editors, and readers feel you are an important part of the magazine – which you are. Receiving letters, yes even problems, from them is surely the most genuine sign of approval any writer could hope to achieve.

Word puzzles

Word puzzles are popular attractions for readers in many magazines. The complexity and nature of published puzzles will reflect the readership and market study answers questions about what kind of word puzzle to compile. There are magazines devoted to nothing else but word puzzles, and on the whole those published are agreeably undemanding, involving nothing more than locating words written in straight lines upwards, downwards, diagonally, from left to right and vice versa in a grid of individual letters. There is virtually no skill required in either devising or solving such puzzles. This being so, the rewards for compilers are small.

If your market is of a specialist interest let the puzzle embrace words relevant to the jargon of the magazine, i.e. boating terms for a sailing magazine or cycling language for one for cyclist readers, adding a 'specially made' flavour to the puzzle as well as making it simpler for the readers to solve. Seasonal puzzles are also popular. This is an easy way to make such a word puzzle:

1 List at least a dozen appropriate words; up to 50 or 60 if the magazine is agreeable.
2 Draw a grid of the required size on squared paper.
3 Write two of the longest words at any position in the grid, interconnecting with a common letter and repeat this as

many times as you can, using words not already on your list if necessary.

4 Continue placing words anywhere in the grid until you have used all on your list.

5 Use a different colour pen, at this stage, to write any letters you like in the blank spaces not used by your 'proper' words.

6 Check that all the words on your list (which will be printed beside the puzzle) exactly match those appearing in the puzzle (that also means being careful not to insert unintentional words when you fill in the blank spaces).

7 Make two top copies of the completed puzzle: one for publication and the other, on which you should circle the listed words, for the editor to try for himself. He won't publish it if you've made any mistakes!

Compiling more challenging word puzzles is fun. For several years I made occasional contributions to a well-known women's magazine's fascinating and highly specialised word puzzle. It consisted of a number of words to be fitted into an irregular crossword pattern; both the words and the pattern varied each month. Although I never discovered how many entries my puzzles were expected to attract I was told that if the numbers fell below 'a minimum figure' they would be rejected. On two occasions they were returned as 'unsuitable' and this kept me on my toes. No doubt I had fallen into the trap of enjoying a particular writing job so much I had temporarily forgotten its purpose: to entertain and intrigue readers in large numbers. Enjoy what you are writing by all means but never let personal satisfaction take precedence over the hard facts of marketing reality. Enjoyment is a bonus.

Crosswords

Many magazines print crosswords and a good many others would like to do so if they could find compilers to provide what they want. Clearly magazines in the latter category are well worth studying. Children's magazines, trade and lesser-known journals are often keen to buy and submissions to these markets are not numerous, giving you a better chance if you are a beginner at crossword-compiling.

If you've ever tried you've probably found writing a few words in a bare block, without any clear idea of where you're going or what you're doing, soon leads to a 'block' of quite another sort – and defeat. A few precepts work wonders:

1 Construct a squared block complete with 'blacks'. Copy one from elsewhere if you wish (copyright resides in clues, not empty blocks) or devise your own. Symmetry is satisfying though not vital but all words must interconnect.

2 Make a list of words that might feature in the complete puzzle; words suitable to the publication, its readers and the 'language' they share.

3 Fill the block with words (see below).

4 Number squares in the block where the solution words are to be entered.

5 Write your clues and number them to match the numbers in the block.

Item (3) is, of course, the most difficult part: 'fill the block with words' sounds easy until you start doing it. Three tips known to experienced compilers are useful:

• The letters E, T, A, O, I, N and S (the most commonly used in the English language) are the best with which to begin words.

• Words with few vowels sit more happily on the left of the block, especially at the top, than elsewhere.

• Be wary about abbreviations, plurals and words ending with vowels other than E.

Compiling crosswords can be addictive and there is no precise list of rules that will make it simple because each crossword is unique. But this is one area where, even if perfection at times seems bafflingly elusive, practice does make perfect. And that is the only solution.

Book reviewing

This is the goal of many writers, especially those who imagine reviewing books means reading what you like, at your own pace, and then getting handsomely paid for writing about it. Alas, it doesn't.

Certainly book reviewing for magazines is a task writers enjoy but consider the following:

• Reviewers must be well read with a wide and varied

knowledge of published books. You cannot intelligently comment on a new book if you cannot 'see' it in its context or genre.

- A review is not merely a summary of the book's story or contents. Its purpose is to tell readers, with your justification, why it is (or is not) of interest and delight.
- Discipline and accuracy are essential. Power-hungry, name-dropping or revenge-seeking reviewers are unemployable.
- Reviewers are hired for their experience, particularly with the relevant magazine or magazine group. The necessary experience will probably be in the fields of writing about books, authors, publishing and the associated general fiction scene. But the more general writing credentials you can present to an editor the better. Virtually all book reviewers hold their positions by editorial invitation rather than by applying for the job, despite official obligations for magazines to advertise vacancies. This doesn't mean the editor's non-journalistic niece gets a soft job solely because she likes a good book occasionally: it simply illustrates the point that someone, insider or freelance, *whose worth and ability are known to the editor*, is the best person for the job.
- It's a time-consuming job. Skimming through chapter headings or rewriting the blurb will not suffice.
- Even high-circulation magazines pay comparatively low fees.

If you are determined to be a published book reviewer try your hand with small-circulation, perhaps local, magazines. You will have to buy the books in the first place and may not get paid much, if anything, for reviewing them but you will have made a start. The reviews will be useful to show editors higher up the publishing scale when you seek a regular reviewing corner of your own in an established magazine and the writing of them will boost your confidence. Practising how to write briefly and concisely is valuable and book reviews are generally short, seldom exceeding five hundred words. Consumer magazines receive quantities of books from publishers eager for the publicity a review can bring and when you work as a regular reviewer the decision of which books to select for review may be made by the features or page editor, or it may even be left in your hands.

Any questions? Yes, become an established magazine reviewer and you *do* keep the books.

Computer games

If you use a word-processor for your work you may find relaxation in playing computer games. Magazines devoted to games-playing compete for readers, while even computer titles of a more serious technical tone generally include at least a section for apparently insatiable games enthusiasts. · Major publishing houses like Haymarket and EMAP and also smaller organisations print games and information about them for the cheaper end of the market and an open door is presented for writers ready and able to join this particular bandwagon. Could you review or invent computer games?

The former is not difficult if you are into the games-playing business, are familiar with the style and characteristics of the genre and know the jargon. The games-playing public eagerly awaits good new releases and when a computer company launches a game, regardless of whether it involves manoeuvring a little man round a complex maze, playing a gentle game of cards or shooting invader starships out of the sky, getting it favourably reviewed in a computer magazine ensures quick profits. With so much enthusiasm for games you would be right in thinking there is fierce competition for writing reviews but most publishers in this field complain that, although they can find potential reviewers who have the right knowledge and background, they seldom come across any who can also *write*. If you are thoroughly acquainted with the world of computer games, enjoy playing them and can write – step right up.

Follow the usual procedure for success in any field: study the magazine you plan to target for the specific computer you can cover. Then practise playing games and write some (private) reviews to test your own style and skill. The editor of your chosen market must be convinced you are a games enthusiast, know what you are talking about and can write objectively in the language he likes.

Experts tell me inventing computer games requires a special flair. Again, manufacturers report few of the games submitted to them are worth developing: lack of originality and imagination are the most common faults. The most well-established publishers of games are to be found in the United

States but in this country and the rest of Europe companies continue to expand in this lucrative market. The games magazine *Ace* (full name *Advanced Computer Entertainment*, a £2.75 monthly) refers to many manufacturers by name and usually gives information about their requirements. You may be one of those dedicated fanatics able to program an exciting new scene of hi-tech moonmen dashing round the stratosphere rescuing mermaids, or football heroes scoring more goals in two minutes than any real player ever did. I have just one plea: if you *do* invent a new computer game and have a software house publish it, please don't send me a copy.

Magazine competitions

When I won a cash prize in a consumer-magazine competition sponsored by Heinz I fell to thinking how well the competition was attuned to likely readers, how popular it must have been and how I could devise different competitions to interest the editor for future issues.

In due course I worked out several competitions of a similar standard and appeal to those already published and began a careful courtship of the editor involved. Would he be interested in seeing what I had to offer? Yes. Could I send or show him some I thought he would like? Yes, but with no promises on his part. Then, when he'd had a chance to consider my submissions a correspondent wrote to the editor asking for a greater variety of competitions to enter. He replied to me – with acceptance of all my competitions, wanting to publish them in successive monthly editions of his magazine. Would I visit him at head office to discuss with some of his suppliers just how the competitions were to be administered? Would I!

This led to a pleasant little writing job that could have lasted longer than it did, had not other more pressing work intervened. It's a task I gladly recommend to any writer with more than a passing interest in entering or compiling competitions as there are many agreeable side-effects. The contests may be simple quizzes but they often take the form of a few questions and answers (generally about the sponsored product) followed by a sentence-completion task. This might be something like 'I love Blogg's Cereal because . . . ' or entrants may be asked to list in preferred order a number of attributes of a particular cleaning product or a company selling cut-price holidays.

Sometimes magazines run competitions with big prizes as definite reader-magnets. These also serve reader-research purposes, the responses giving the publishers an idea into what readers want and in what numbers. These competitions may also be the work of outside contributors, especially those known to have experience in this field.

Editors are always open to competition suggestions but be sure to do all your thinking before making your initial approach: there are many points to be settled. Is your proposed competition to be solved by luck, perseverance, knowledge, or with what combination of the three? Is the solution to be printed on another page in the same issue or are there to be prizes for submitting the correct solution? Where will the prizes come from? Who will judge the entries and despatch the prizes?

Once in the competition frame of mind you may like to enter a few trade contests yourself. Forms are generally freely displayed in large supermarkets or in the magazines available at their check-out counters. This is good training in writing with economy and aptness and can be highly profitable. I know people who have won cars, overseas holidays and even houses just by completing sentences in a few suitable words. Will you be the next to do so?

Arts and entertainment

Do you love music, fine art, theatre or films? All entertainment organisers crave publicity and that means editors may be willing to consider previews of forthcoming events. Regional magazines, for instance, are often happy to preview drama or arts presentations soon to occur in their areas. A particular play may be scheduled for the local opera house or the work of a much acclaimed artist will shortly be on show at a nearby art gallery. If you have good contacts in the theatre or arts world you could be just the person to write magazine previews. As usual, contact the editor with your credentials (you are not likely to make much progress without any as this is seldom a field for complete beginners) and ask if he is interested. This job attracts competition, not least because of free tickets and allied perks, so your first task may not be covering a very sophisticated event but it will give you experience for when greater challenges come your way.

To write a preview of a particular event you must ensure your copy is directed to a dated issue of the magazine, so mention this point clearly in your covering letter even if the timing has been fully discussed with the editor prior to submission.

Fillers

The widespread (almost universal) use of modern technology has revolutionised the technique of laying out magazine pages. With a few simple key strokes columns can be moved, headings resized, pix cropped and everything adapted to suit the page editor's precise requirements. The results can look neater and better than in the old pre-tech days but the change has not been without casualties. With everything so easily lined up to fill its allotted space, those little gaps so useful for small fillers have virtually disappeared. But we writers can turn this apparent loss to our advantage by upgrading small items – old 'filler' material – into snippets with a dignity and place of their own.

You like verse? Short quotations in 'boxed' format (that simply means submitting them enclosed inside a ruled box) can add variety to pages rather heavy on text and are popular as regularly published items.

Palindromes fascinate me. Do they do the same for other people? Yes, I discovered, when I started a running-filler on the topic in a general-interest magazine. I wrote a short and deliberately provocative item quoting the longest palindrome I could find at the time:

ABLE WAS I ERE I SAW ELBA

Did anyone know a longer one? Entries flooded in and over the next few issues my original 19 letter sample grew to:

TO PREDICATE GO GET A CIDER POT (25)

and:

TO CLARET ALAS IT IS A LATERAL COT (27)

I thought this must be the end of the line, but no. An enterprising reader clinched it with:

SATAN OSCILLATE MY METALLIC SONATAS – an incredible 31 letters.

At the same time I introduced date palindromes. Ordinary ones are quite common and I reminded readers that, for instance, the 29th of every month in 1992 (except October and December) reads backwards as well as forwards: 29–4–92, 29–6–92, etc. But there was something extra about the 18th of January in 1981. This was a *super*palindrome year for 18–1–81 not only reads the same backwards as forwards but (in suitably written figures) upside down as well. The same happened in August (18–8–81) and November (18–11–81) that year. Who, I invited readers, could work out what the next superpalindromic date would be? The response was not long in coming[1] and the whole topic provoked lively letters to the editor.

With that he decided to call a halt. I use the term 'running-filler' because that's exactly what it was; the topic soon running out of steam when readers who wanted to contribute had done so and there was nothing further to add. (Of course if you know any palindromes longer than 31 letters . . .)

Quotations both serious and humorous can also lighten a page. A colleague contributed an amusing or clever quotation to a weekly magazine for five or six years under the title 'I wish I'd said . . . ' And children's sayings never fail to bring smiles to readers' lips.

Humour is always welcome providing it is suited to the taste and style of the magazine. If you're interested further in writing comedy here is an organisation you might like to contact:

Comedy Writers' Association of Great Britain, Ken Rock, 61 Parry Road, Ashmore Park, Wolverhampton WV11 2PS. Tel: 0902 722729.

I've found bits and pieces that have come my way well worth jotting down for use as filler material. Like these:

Seen on the noticeboard of a Northumberland golf club: 'The ladies section will be glad to play the gentlemen when they have nothing on.'

From a weekly newspaper: 'John and Mary would like to

[1] January 10th 2001: 10–1–01.

thank family, friends and neighbours for the presents, cards and flowers received on the arrival of their twin daughters. We would also like to thank the midwife and the vicar for making it all possible.'

To a writer, nothing heard, read or seen is ever wasted and even the smallest titbits can be put to good use.

Letters to the editor

I'm sad when I hear some writers saying writing letters to the editor, letters for publication, is a waste of time. 'It's the last resort,' they sigh, 'because they won't pay me anything even if my letters are published.' There are at least two faults in such despairing argument. Far from being the last resort of the otherwise unpublished, writing a letter to the editor focuses the mind on a single aspect of a single theme and is a valuable exercise in the twin disciplines of conciseness and relevance. Nor is it always unpaid as the many dedicated letter writers to magazines will confirm. Perhaps, by the very nature of their self-imposed task, we should consider such enterprising and busy folk to be following a hobby, while 'proper' writers engaged in work of greater substance than letters-to-the-editor prefer to think of themselves in more serious vein. But what's the difference? Whatever the length, weight or subject matter of our end-product and wherever it appears in a magazine's editorial pages, it is a valid piece of published work of which we may be proud.

Those wishing to write letters to the editor need to study their intended markets as closely as anyone writing longer pieces. Brevity is essential with as few as fifty words often the average length of published letters. You need to make your mark without any preamble and encompass all you want to say in the word limit allowed or your most important point may be cut. (And that means, of course, the letter won't be published at all.)

Imagine reading a magazine and finding a letter-to-the-editor that you simply must read out to those around you; perhaps it makes you laugh or annoys you or confirms your opinion about something or evokes happy memories or gives you some information you need or comments on something you read in last week's issue. These are the types of letters that are published and the sort you could be submitting for publication. You may get paid (magazines usually indicate their intentions, sometimes only paying for the best published at the time) or you may receive some small present in thanks. Frequently general and women's titles offer gifts or cash payments for the best letter received by a certain date and written about a specified topic. This, of course, is one of the many editorial ploys to encourage regular purchase.

When editors invite you to give your own views or relate your experiences you can be sure it is not just to assure themselves of a swollen postbag: it is another of the publisher's methods of researching what his readers want and what sort of people they are. What could be more direct than the invitation to 'write and tell us'? Make your reply one of those chosen for publication and both you and the editor are happy. Whether you are paid in cash or kind, or not at all, if your letter is published in a mass-selling periodical or a small one in the area where you live, one reward probably coming your way is the response from other readers – and that is always worth having.

Resist letting success in this field go to your head. Give editors the suspicion you are engaging in writing letters as more than just an interested and observant reader of their publication (you might, horror, even be making a part-time job out of it) and they could turn your offerings away with nary a glance. The answer is to write letters that editors know other readers will like reading and to cast your net wide. The wider you spread it the more your market study will extend and the sounder your judgement of markets will be for submitting other work.

When you've made your mark

When you've achieved success with some of the challenges above you will find you enjoy being an IDA. But the most exciting task comes when you are asked to stand in for an absent staff member. Some time ago I learned to watch out for the pregnant! In due course there's bound to be a gap on the staff, a vacancy sure to last some months, and an IDA is the ideal person to fill it. Such an arrangement can suit all parties: the editor, who knows he can rely on you and your work, the absent staff member who can take time off without feeling she has left her colleagues floundering, and you, who have been hoping for an opportunity to spread your wings.

Other staff absences due to holidays or illness present chances for the enterprising freelance who has shown all the important IDA qualities. And sometimes absent staff, for a number of reasons, don't come back . . .

Beyond the magazine world

Most writing tasks have a happy knack of leading to others, which makes the whole business so satisfactory. Turn your eyes to further assignments outside the business of magazines. Here are ten off-beat writing jobs worth pursuing:

- Company histories for local firms.
- Advertising features for area or regional newspapers.
- Brochures and leaflets for hotels, holiday or coach companies.
- Charity appeals for fund-raisers.
- Notices and posters for schools and libraries.
- Booklets for walkers and owners of historic houses.
- Speeches for public figures who are not writers.
- CVs for job-seekers.
- Anniversary brochures for local businesses.
- Preparing applications for people seeking grants, etc.

Using your imagination

I know a lady in North Wales who has a passion for short verses of the type often found in greetings cards. She collects them in albums under various headings: children, nostalgia, animals and pets, the countryside, and so on. One day when she was thumbing through her collection she thought she could write verses equally acceptable to card recipients, if not better. She took note of the publishers' names on the back of the cards and began researching further afield. A helpful newsagent put her on to *Greetings Magazine*, the bi-monthly trade periodical for retailers, wholesalers and stationers (Lema Publishing Co., Unit No.1, Queen Mary's Avenue, Watford, Herts. WD4 8PP. Tel: 0923 250909) and she now sees her own verses appearing regularly in greetings cards of all types. She has made a hobby that interests her into a small part-time occupation bringing in some welcome cheques.

Could you be an IDA? Of all writers they probably have the most fun.

7

Overseas markets

Curiosity about other people and the way they live is the lifeblood of writers. Readers at a distance in their own lands want to know about us, our country and our lives and they want to read what we write. This is keenly recognised by magazine publishers overseas whose titles welcome acceptable freelance submissions from other countries simply because they are *different*. Childhood deafness, for instance, is an affliction that knows no national or international boundaries yet an article on dealing with it written for, let us say, an American magazine by a British writer will certainly take a different viewpoint from one written by an American. It's not that one will necessarily be better than the other but that, in the case of writing for overseas publications, distance lends the enchantment of looking through new eyes.

Don't let's forget reality; enchantment is fine, but please note that essential word 'acceptable' in the previous paragraph. All the parameters of market study obtain and if you don't want to waste time, effort and money on winging unwanted words round the world it is vital to observe them.

So always acquire sample magazines for study when you intend to submit your work overseas – indeed, as I should emphasise, *especially* when you intend to submit overseas. At the same time ask for any writers' guidelines the magazines may issue, as most do so. If you have any friends in the chosen country beg them to send you back numbers but, if you don't know anyone who will do so, simply write to the title of your choice and ask for them. The cover prices quoted will be in their currency so remember to check the operative exchange rate. Include adequate International Reply Coupons (available from any UK post office) which the receiver simply uses to buy postage stamps in his country s currency when he replies to you. Never send envelopes for return bearing UK stamps to countries that do not use them. Not only is this wasteful, it tells the receiving editor you have little knowledge of his country: hardly the best impression to give him when you want him to buy your copy.

Most foreign embassies in the UK are happy to provide information about magazines published in their countries. *Whitaker's Almanack* and other reference books detail embassy addresses. Discover the correct name of your contact as most overseas markets appreciate the personal touch. But also remember the holders of positions on magazines may change and, as the time lapse between your enquiry and eventual submission will probably take longer than the same procedure would here, address your intended recipient by a job title as well as a personal name. For topical or timed articles you want to appear in a magazine on a particular date, work backwards from it to choose when to post your copy. Most overseas magazines work to publishing time schedules similar to those observed in this country but it is wise to exceed them. So for an article you hope the editor will accept for publication in the July edition, say, of his monthly title, you should post your copy by Christmas, if not before. This will allow ample time for him to contact you about anything that might arise: queries, requests for elucidation or expansion on particular points, further information, pictures or anything else he might want.

Of course your market study will take note of your potential title's special interests and likely (or stated) taboos but never feel overseas periodicals will be happy with anything but the very best you can provide.

All your copy must offer First Rights of the country you are submitting to. That still means your article may have been published in the UK, selling First British Rights, but no others. As trade with the European Union develops magazine publishers are talking of merging the reproduction rights of various countries under a single 'European' label. Already several organisations market what are known as 'pan-European' titles, i.e. the same magazines sold in their own languages, sometimes with different titles, in several EU countries. But national differences in what readers want make this less easy than it sounds and, for the moment at least, virtually all copy originally written for publication in one country needs rewriting before it is acceptable in another.

Notwithstanding this (which we writers can hardly consider a problem) I envisage a significant increase in the pan-European method of marketing and recommend writers with an eye on regular future sales to follow its development; the problems will be solved, because that is the only reason problems exist, and we cannot be far from the time when contributors simply deliver copy to their nearest office – in their home country – to submit to titles in as many European countries as participate in the scheme.

It is always worth discovering as much as you can about the country you wish to submit to. Fiction writers know and understand this precept but sometimes non-fiction writers fall into the trap of thinking that as distant readers are out of sight they can also be out of mind. For general information about a country the Department of Trade and Industry's guides provide valuable background reading; copies are free and obtainable on request from any of the DTI's eight regional offices or from Ashdown House, 123 Victoria Street, London SW1E 6RB. Tel: 071–215 5000. Never forget the golden rule of marketing: you are writing for *readers*, not editors or publishers. Anything that helps you understand who those readers are and what sort of lives they lead must be beneficial. So don't skimp reader-research, and then remind yourself that quality of research must be followed by quality writing.

Payment varies enormously, is not always listed in reference guides and should be ascertained before submission. Even magazines paying little are generally worth dealing with, particularly at the start of your writing career. They sometimes present opportunities to expand overseas sales to higher-paying markets in due course. Low paying markets also attract less competition than the high payers; only you can decide how much your copy is worth in terms of cash profit, so you may have to balance the expense in mailing overseas with the less easily costed advantages of gaining a foothold at the bottom of the ladder.

Some magazines, particularly in the US, furnish writers with an advanced list of themes to be covered in forthcoming issues. These are enormously helpful and can save fruitless effort in the preparation of copy on a topic already in the pipeline. They also provide useful extra guidance to market requirements, reflecting considered editorial policy.

Even apparently trivial matters sometimes count: many American magazines still use the 'old' quarto paper size (11″ by 8¼″) so do not submit copy on A4 paper to a market that doesn't use it. You may have difficult obtaining quarto nowadays and have to cut it for yourself, but an American editor finding A4 won't fit into his filing system may feel it can't be worth his attention if the writer is ignorant of his office's most basic needs.

Writing in English

Do markets overseas present an insuperable problem when published in their own language, while you only write in English? Not necessarily. In general there are four methods of selling to overseas markets and, whichever you choose, the language problem is easily overcome. I outline them below in my personal order of preference:

1 Do-it-yourself. This involves doing all the work yourself, including market study, querying potential editors and selling to them as well (of course) as researching, writing and presenting your copy, with illustrations if required. You may be asked to contribute to translation costs or even to meet them in full. But sometimes, depending on the status and strength of the market, the receiving magazine bears all such expenses. There are undoubted advantages in a DIY approach, not least of which is that all the proceeds are yours. More importantly, nothing quite replaces the personal touch and working this way may establish what could be valuable future contacts. But you do have to be patient as finding the right market can be a lengthy process. You also have to bear all the costs.

2 Hands across the sea. Find a friend in your targeted country to help and share the burdens of market research and postal expenses. Someone with knowledge or at least interest in the writing business will be most helpful and the ideal person could be a writer trying to sell to markets in this country. If you write about similar or related topics you could find such a partnership of mutual benefit. A good friend can save you time and money *there*, but don't forget the time and money you will have to expend on your friend's copy *here*. When your friend can tell you of markets not listed in any guidebook, never written about in writers' magazines, virtually unknown here and yet longing for freelance copy of the very type you want to write – when that happens this method of selling overseas beats all others. Maybe your friend can also help if trans-

lation into another tongue is involved. But perfect fluency
is essential, as any professional translator will tell you, so
be careful before accepting such an offer. Inadequate
translation can ravage all your hard work and will
inevitably spoil what might have been a valuable friend-
ship.

3 Syndication. This can be the least troublesome way to
sell overseas and frees you from any translation problems.
If you just want to concentrate on writing and let someone else cope with marketing and all its associated time-
consuming tasks this is the way to work. Lists of
syndication agents are to be found in the pages of the
Writers' & Artists' Yearbook but it pays to be sure of the
terms of agencies before handing over your work. They
also vary widely in translation fees; some charge a lot,
others nothing, one may act promptly while another
merely adds your copy to a heap already gathering dust,
and a few always announce your work needs rewriting –
for a fee. Syndication agents want ideas rather than
finished pieces. When they are interested in your suggested topic and its likely treatment you just write it up
and hand it over.

How can you distinguish the goodies from the baddies?
There is nothing like the recommendation of a writing
friend who has dealt with an agency you are hoping to
use. But really good ones (and there are several) have
sufficient clients already and may not be willing to accept
any more. It is important to them that you should have
plenty of copy to market and that you can keep it coming.
The one-off article or even the just-now-and-then piece is
unlikely to interest top-notch agencies when they have
clients on their books who provide them with regular
bread-and-butter. To succeed in syndication you should
aim to *be* such a client . . . Selling to the growing number
of pan-European titles, as mentioned earlier in this chapter, is itself a type of syndication and one which could
have a bright future. See also Syndication in Chapter 12.

4 Literary agents.   Find a literary agent who will do all
the overseas marketing work for you. Generally this is
not easy for non-fiction writers and if you have no proven
track-record you may find it impossible. A friend of mine
approached a literary agent wanting him to sell non-

fiction to magazines. He looked at her in some bewilderment and told her, politely but with resignation, that she was wasting his time as he very seldom dealt with non-fiction material for magazines. At her hesitation he amended his 'very seldom' to 'virtually never' – and she didn't persist. Perhaps he guessed her heart wasn't with her head in asking him to sell copy for her. Should you venture along a similar path you may have better luck. Frankly, I think we freelance non-fiction writers do better without agents anyway.

Markets

The most reliable reference guides to overseas markets are *Writers' & Artists' Yearbook* and *Willing's Press Guide* but even the most recent editions are, being annual publications, inevitably out of date before they reach your hands. This fact highlights the importance of personal market study, for which there is no substitute, lists and guidebooks (even this one) notwithstanding. In these pages it is only possible to give details of a few overseas markets in a handful of countries but perhaps that is no disadvantage for freelance writers. Any less-than-comprehensive list has to be selective, inevitably restricting some potential contributors and falsely encouraging others. I cannot know the writing ambitions and abilities of everyone reading this, so I mention the following markets with three injunctions:

- Details are published solely to whet the appetite.
- In no way are they substitutes for personal market study and research.
- Market information is correct at the time I write this but may not still be so when you read it.

I list several European countries in order of their general use of English and add brief information of some sample markets, many of them not referred to in conventional market guides.

Ireland

The only European country presenting no language problem to freelance writers in English is curiously neglected on this side of the Irish Sea. Opportunities abound both in Northern

Ireland and in the Republic of Ireland, the former generally offering higher fees but the latter wider in scope for free-lances.

Church of Ireland Gazette, 36 Bachelor's Walk, Lisburn, Co. Antrim BT28 1XN. Tel: 0846 675743. Items and short articles of 600–1000 words on general and religious interest. Weekly. 20p.

Ireland's Own, North Main Street, Wexford. Tel: 053 22155. An old-established magazine wanting articles for Irish readers at home and overseas. Welcomes suggestions for new features, jokes, riddles, funny stories, etc. Publishes special issues for Christmas and St Patrick's Day (17 March). Weekly. 40p.

Holland

Luckily for writers in English, a high proportion of Dutch folk read and speak English and many of them regularly read magazines published on both sides of the English Channel. The Royal Netherlands Embassy (38 Hyde Park Gate, London SW7 5DP. Tel: 071–584 5040) issues a comprehensive media list of Dutch periodicals and there are pages of them detailed in *Willing's Press Guide*. The magazine business is thriving, sophisticated and large, dominated by giant publishers VNU who also control interests in printing and delivery. Further information about VNU's enterprise is available from Admedia UK, Glenthorne House, Hammersmith Grove, London W6 0LG. Tel: 071–741 1333.

Germany

The magazine business is holding its own in Denmark, Belgium, France and rather less so in Italy despite recessionary and other pressures.

German magazines have taken an enormous leap forward in the last few years. Leading periodicals employ their own translators of anything they want to buy that is not written in German. The periodical publishing business is huge, second in the European Union only to our own, and publications regularly accept copy written in almost any language from all over the world. As I write, the general translation fee (which writers are expected to pay) varies from £40 to £75 per

thousand words. But if you throw your hands up in horror at
this, remember that compared to the majority of British titles
German magazines pay high fees: the equivalent of £250 per
1000 words is not unusual.

Writing for German magazines is little different from writing for British ones if your normal standards are first-rate.
They expect and only accept top-quality work, thoroughly
researched, impeccably presented and efficiently offered.
They tend to pay by lineage rather than by the number of
words and are known for paying promptly, although not all
will maintain this high reputation. They are well organised
and assume their contributors are the same.

The Embassy of the Federal Republic of Germany (23
Belgrave Square, London SW1X 8PZ. Tel: 071–235 5033) will
either supply lists of the country's periodicals or pass your
request on to other sources of information.

Frau Im Spiegel, Dr Julius Leberstrasse 3–7, Lübeck.
Published weekly for women from 20 to 45. Welcomes
British tradition, royalty, celebrities, etc. UK representative
Gruner & Jahr, 7 Cavendish Square, London W1M 9HA.

Das Neue Blatt, Heinrich Bauer Verlag, Postfach 10 04 14,
Burchardstrasse 11, W 2000. Hamburg 1. General interest
weekly for older women, publishing a wide range of
articles.

Quick, Postfach 20 17 28, 8000 München 2. Weekly in-
depth periodical dealing with social, political and moral
issues of worldwide interest. Interviews and illustrations
wanted.

Spain

In Spain, with its thriving tourist industry attracting large
numbers of English-speaking visitors, some thirty magazines
are published regularly in English as well as several hundreds
published in Spanish. Virtually all the English-language
periodicals welcome freelance submissions. I once found a
copy of one on a seat in a Madrid park and contributed to it
regularly for the next three years. It is worth remembering
that more than 50,000 Britons live in Spain, most of them over
retirement age. What do such folk want to read about? How
to settle in a new country in their later years, the best ways of

investing money, where and how to buy property, explanations of local and national customs, reassurance that all is well back home . . . the list presents potential writers for Spanish magazines with plenty of choice. (See also the end of this chapter about writing for expatriates.)

Anyone who has ever been to Spain knows life seldom proceeds at more than a gentle pace and writers vow the Spanish Post Office is a law unto itself. This is part of its charm but it can protract editorial queries and replies over many months or even years, so be sure to extend lead times when wanting to sell copy for a dated future edition.

Speak Up, 185–1, 08021 Barcelona, Spain. A monthly title for young adult learners of English. Generally welcomes lively but carefully written articles about modern and current topics.

USA

The United States is the first market that comes to most writers' minds when they think of selling overseas and for the majority it is the best place to sell to. If you take it seriously you need the two most authoritative American market guides published for potential contributors. Both are available from British bookshops or may be ordered directly. They are:

Writer's Market, F. & W. Publications Inc., 1507 Dana Avenue, Cincinnati, OH 45207. Details over 4000 publications covering fiction, drama and small items as well as non-fiction. Each annual update lists hundreds of new markets and the current edition is subtitled 'Where & how to sell what you write'. It includes an enormous amount of information about rights, research, freelance business matters, alternative opportunities, photographs and slides, postage, querying editors and fees. A huge section on consumer magazines covering every conceivable topic provides information, usually in great detail, often with editorial quotes about precise requirements. $26.95 plus $4.00 post and packing.

The Writer's Handbook, The Writer, Inc., 120 Boylston Street, Boston, MA 02116. This invaluable reference book embraces the names, addresses, type of material wanted, rates of pay – and much more – of over 3000 markets ranging from general interest, regional and city publications, family, lifestyle, environment, religion, health, business, college, literary and little magazines. Also included are no fewer than 110 chapters by the world's most successful authors, editors and literary agents. Distinguished writers share their experiences and discuss what worked for them. The creative process, inspiration, persistence, reaching your reader and many more topics are fully explored and explained. $29.95 plus postage.

Also strongly recommended are:

The Writer's Guide to Conquering the Magazine Market by Connie Emerson, Writer's Digest Books, F. & W. Publications Inc., 1507 Dana Avenue, Cincinnati, OH 45207.   The author has sold hundreds of articles to a wide selection of magazines and her sales consistently outnumber rejections by more than 20 to 1. Learn more professional techniques, tailored specifically for the American markets, and a systematic approach to selling your own work. $17.95 or £9.95.

Chicago Review, 5801 S. Kenwood, Chicago IL 60637. Publishes innovative features on a wide variety of topics and welcomes both solicited and unsolicited manuscripts. Address non-fiction to Mark Morrisson. No simultaneous submissions. No strict length requirements.

Housewife Writer's Forum, PO Box 780, Lyman, WY 82937. For busy women (and men) who share a commitment to writing while juggling home life and family responsibilities. Many readers are working or single mothers, women with adult children or no children, and retired folk. Ranks verve and emotion ahead of linguistic gymnastics and looks for clear, concise and vivid language. Writing style should be lucid and to the point. In-depth non-fiction should be under 1500 words. Wants well-researched articles, practical tips and interviews/profiles of writers who have been successful. Personal experience articles are wanted offering practical advice on how to overcome problems or break into particular markets. Query first with ideas. 'Confessions of a Housewife-Writer' (200 words maximum), humour and fillers also wanted. Lindy Capel is Articles Editor.

Wants First North American Serial Rights or One Time Rights.

America's Equestrian, PO Box 249, 114 West Hills Road, Huntington Station, NY 1174. A six-times a year informative publication for the horse enthusiast, amateur, professional, competitor, business person and horse lover. Wants articles and photographs (colour or black and white 5" by 7" preferred) with full explanatory captions. Payment $100 to $150 per article of 1300 to 2000 words with extra for pix.

Cricket Magazine, PO Box 300, Peru, IL 61354. A 64-page literary monthly for children age 6 to 14 which includes articles as well as fiction and poetry written by the world's best children's authors. Wants to reach as many children's illustrators and authors as possible for original contributions but standards are very high and only top-quality material is accepted. Non-fiction requirements (200 to 1200 words): biography, history, science, technology, natural history, social science, geography, foreign culture, travel, adventure and sports. A short bibliography must be attached to all non-fiction. Please do not query first. Speculative submissions always considered but replies can take 12 weeks. Address to Submissions Editor.

alive now!, 1908 Grand Avenue, PO Box 189, Nashville, TN 37202–0189. (note the lower-case title). Published for those struggling to be alive to the God who is living and active, for those who want to grow and to work out their faith in the contemporary scene. Wants writing that is hopeful in tone from writers who deal honestly and frankly with problems – theirs, the church's and the world's. Material should invite reflection, prayer and action. Keep it short and remember some circulation is below the Equator so don't necessarily equate Easter with spring or Christmas with winter. Be creative but not self-centred in good writing from a Christian standpoint. Provides list of projected themes. Usual payment $15 to $20.

The Georgia Review, The University of Georgia, Athens, Georgia 30602. One of America's most widely read journals of arts and letters, published every quarter by the

University of Georgia and featuring non-fiction (among other sections) to appeal 'across disciplinary lines'. Draws material from a wide range of cultural interests including literature, history, philosophy, politics, film, music and the visual arts. Non-fiction should be informed articles against a broad perspective. Not interested in scholarly articles narrow in focus and/or over-burdened with footnotes. The ideal article is provocative and thesis-orientated to engage both the intelligent general reader and the specialist. No unsolicited work considered during June, July or August. Payment $35 per printed page for First North American Serial Rights.

Mennonite Publishing House, 616 Walnut Avenue, Scottdale, PA 15683–1999. Five magazines sharing one address. All buy one-time rates only but payment varies.

Christian Living. Ten issues per year. Seeks articles related to spirituality, community and family. Wants pieces that connect the arts to one of these areas, have cross-cultural dimensions or simply tell a good story. Be concise, include lots of anecdotes and examples, avoid jargon and focus on one topic per article. Queries or complete manuscripts invited. Good black and white photos helpful.

Gospel Herald. A weekly needing 700–1500 word articles on Christian doctrine, life and service. Short succinct pieces of scriptural exposition reporting and analysing trends in the Mennonite Church.

On the Line. Published monthly for children age 10 to 14. Buys articles of 350–1200 words to help them handle problems, to live up to their potential, to learn about nature, art, music, poetry and human relationships, to help them accept other races and cultures as their equals and to make the message of the Bible attractive. Also wants puzzles, quizzes and cartoons.

Purpose. Monthly in weekly parts needing anecdotal fillers and articles written in a terse fast-moving style for older youth and adults of all ages. Articles should show Christians putting their faith to work, help readers in beliefs and decision-making, stress Church loyalty and community duties, emphasise hobbies, nature, travel, art, science and seasonal topics from a Christian perspective and inspire interest in other people and cultures.

With. Published eight times a year for ages 15 to 18. In keeping with the Mennonite commitment it needs articles of from 600–1600 words dealing with any facet of youth life: how-to pieces about relationships with the opposite sex, peer relationships, lifestyle, ethics, etc. Humour is also welcome.

The New Press, 53–35 Hollis Court Blvd, Flushing NY 11365. A literary quarterly publishing some articles (among fiction and poetry) which should be accessible to an intelligent reader and are chosen for literary merit and reading pleasure. Article topics: personal, political and social commentary, writers and writing, poetics, revelatory and informative. General preferences: sensitivity to human relationships and needs. No hatred or glorification of violence. Suitable humour welcome.

Chips off the Writer's Block, Wanda Windham, Editor, PO Box 83371, Los Angeles, CA 90083–0371. How-to articles on all aspects of writing. Inspirational/motivation/working writer pieces. Personal experiences: first sale, moving to bigger markets, etc. Always open to new columns and ideas. Submit a personal-experience article or an informal essay. If more experienced, do some research and show us 'how to'.

St Anthony Messenger, 1615 Republic Street, Cincinnati, OH 45210–1298. General-interest family-orientated Catholic magazine. Types of articles wanted: Church and religion, marriage, family and parenting, social, inspirational, psychological, profiles and interviews. Examples: 'Helping kids from the inside out', 'Fighting abortion with PR', 'Racism through the eyes of a child', 'Recipe for a happy marriage'.

L.A. Parent Magazine, Jack Bierman, Editor, PO Box 3204, Burbank, CA 91504. Needs articles on child development, education, parents and crafts.

Seattle's Child, PO Box 22578, Seattle, WA 98122. Needs features on parents and child care, consumer tips, etc.

Iowa Woman, PO Box 680, Iowa City, IA 52244.
Quarterly rarely publishing work by men. Personal voice,
intelligence and good writing essential. Possible topics
(from long list): successful Iowa businesswomen, women
in poverty, women married 50 years to same man, older
women as role models, women who began writing in
mid-life.

Innisfree, PO Box 277, Manhattan Beach, CA 90266.
Home-grown informal literary magazine of professional
quality. New and unpublished writers welcome. Wants
articles, memoirs, travelogues and descriptions of different countries and cultures. No political or religious sensa-
tionalism.

Canada

When writers on the British side of the Atlantic look west-
wards they tend to forget Canadian magazines. That must
explain why Canadian editors receive so little material from
over here. There are about 1000 magazines published across
the country, most of them well written and upbeat. The great
US market is not far away so Canadian periodicals have to be
tough to survive. For the best list of markets you need the
Canadian Writers Guide, 195 All State Parkway, Markham,
Ontario L3R 4T8.

Canadian, 111 Avenue Road, Suite 801, Toronto, Canada
M5R 3J8. The in-flight publication of Canadian Airlines
International. Likes travel and business-interest pieces
1000–1500 words. Payment is on acceptance but varies.

Canadian Author, Suite 500, 275 Slater Street, Ottawa,
Ontario, Canada K1P 5B9. For Canadian writers of all
ages at all levels of experience; 95 per cent freelance
written. Interviews, informative and how-to articles.
1000–2500 words. No personal, lightweight writing
experiences or fillers. Send for sample copy and writer's
guidelines.

Good Times, 5148 St Lawrence Boulevard, Montreal,
Quebec H2T 1R8. Published ten times a year for older
and mostly retired readers; 1000–1500 words. Welcomes
colour slides. Write for sample copy and guidelines.

Canadian Stamp News, 103 Lakeshore Road, Suite 202, St Catharines, Ontario, Canada L2N 2T6. Fortnightly magazine welcoming articles with pix on stamp collecting news, rare stamps, etc. Ask for guidelines. Pays on publication.

Australia

Submitting to Australian magazines used to be the least favourite way writers in other countries liked to spend their time. Often there were long delays, if you were lucky, and an apparently endless future of nil response from your targeted magazine if you weren't. Things have improved since those bad old days (a few fellow-writers will disagree with me) but even now dealing with many Australian periodicals takes a lot of time . . . But if you have the patience to sell to Australia you can do well although standards of payment are generally modest.

Australian Magazines is an Australian guide book of similar style to our *Writers' & Artists' Yearbook*. Further information is available from the Press and Public Relations Officer, Australian High Commission, Australia House, Strand, London WC2B 4LA.

Gourmet Traveller, Australian Consolidated Press, 54 Park Street, Sidney, New South Wales 2000. What you're eating according to where you happen to be is the basic theme of this glossy monthly. Illustrations welcome and payment 'by negotiation'.

Golden Years, PO Box 537, Melbourne. Likes articles mainly suited to the needs and tastes of retired people. Interesting short pieces always welcomed.

New Zealand

With a widely scattered population of less than 3½ million New Zealand supports a lively press including more than 600 magazines. They cover topics from accountancy to yachting and present excellent marketing opportunities to observant writers in the UK. A booklet including only brief details of a small selection is provided by the New Zealand High Commission, New Zealand House, Haymarket, London SW1Y 4TQ. Tel:

071–930 8422, but is well worth acquiring as it contains much other useful media information.

NZ Woman's Weekly, Private Bag, Dominion Road, Auckland 3. A popular weekly with some affinities to similar publications in the UK.

Straight Furrow, PO Box 715, Wellington. Published fortnightly, this farming publication has a wide readership.

Bits & Bytes, PO Box 9870, Newmarket, Auckland. Every month (except January) for computer users.

The expatriate market

As the number of Britons living overseas increases, is there a corresponding growth of magazines published specially for them? Yes and no. Many titles, such as *Island Gazette* in the Canaries and *The Algarve*, accept work from local writers only but periodicals issued by the several organisations existing to help expatriates, temporary expatriates and potential expatriates, circulate in the UK as well as overseas and generally welcome contributions from writers resident here. **Nexus**, the magazine of Expat Network (International House, 500 Purley Way, Croydon CR0 4NZ. Tel: 081–760 5100) has special appeal to job-hunters. Its worldwide distribution embraces many different viewpoints and cultures, giving freelance contributors so wide a scope it may at first be difficult to see the wood for the trees. As always, query before starting any serious planning. On the whole expatriate titles are slow to get off the ground, especially when they try to be all things to all people, and many have a tenuous hold on life.

Among other magazines published in this country are the following:

Expat Newsline, H. & S. Associates, Barclays Bank Building, High Street, Chepstow, Gwent NP6 5QX. Tel: 0291 627015.

Home & Away, Expats International Ltd, 29 Lacon Road, East Dulwich, London SE22 9HE. Tel: 081–299 4986.

The Expatriate, First Market Intelligence, 56a Rochester Row, Westminster, London SW1P 1JU. Tel: 071–834 9192.

The whole world . . .

Japan, Taiwan, Korea, China, Hong Kong, Singapore, the Philippines, Malaysia . . . what we think of as the Far East stretches a long way and encompasses many very different lands. That means, in a writer's terms, many different *readers*. And what about the rest of the world? Wherever people live and read there will be markets for writers. As far as we are concerned, oysters have a lot to answer for.

8
Interviewing

Magazine readers want to read about *people* more than anything else. A survey of the contents of 100 magazines of various types including women's, general, hobby, entertainment and trade magazines shows more than 75 per cent of editorial space features the lives, occupations, work and individual accounts of people with stories to tell. That last point is crucial in the business of interviewing – which is not the same as writing *about* someone. The latter is often called a 'profile' and may have a valid place in a magazine but an interview is as 'live' as any written piece on a page can be. An interviewer's job is to make readers feel they have *met and talked with* the interviewee.

Keen observation of the art of the live interview leads me to believe top-rate interviewers are born with some natural ability. That is not to say the craft can't be learned and polished as those few 'experts', and they are few in number, agree. This is particularly the case when considering written interviews which prove so popular with magazine readers.

As with all other forms of writing, the technique of interviewing follows a coherent pattern: an idea, research, preparation, the job itself and the write-up, perhaps with pix. Near the beginning of this sequence comes the most important part of the whole task, *selling* the interview. All these points are considered in this chapter, together with the one frequently worrying newcomers when they remember they only have one crack at the interview: can I do a good job?

Some folk are born with a greater depth of sympathy than others. John may by nature be more perceptive than Jack, Jean shrewder than Jane, Anne more experienced in life than Tom. Wherever you fit into such a pattern of human faculties and frailties, acquiring a good interview technique involves building on your abilities and strengthening your weaknesses. A good interviewer feels comfortable at the interview, relaxed (or with the appearance of being relaxed) and able to make the interviewee feel at ease. Without apparent effort the

interviewer sets the tone of that special one-to-one relationship that is apparent the minute we meet anyone for the first
time: will we get on well together? He (I say 'he' with 'she'
also in mind, of course) will conduct the interview with
genuine pleasure even if it is just a job of work to be done.

You may note I have mentioned the *appearance* of being
relaxed and *without apparent effort*: although not every interviewer can summon tranquil feelings to order and first-time
nerves insist on vexing us all, I have found the determined
disregarding of such unwelcome emotions sends them packing with great speed as soon as the interview begins Then it
is conducted with genuine pleasure. So if you fear you lack
the courage to interview anyone, let alone those well-known
people magazine readers want to know about, take heart.
Forget timidity and all will be well. Remember, too, neither
the readers not the interviewee need know anything about the
secret weapons you have already put to good use long before
the interview takes place . . .

The purpose of the interview

Before you begin it is wise to be honest about the purpose of
conducting the interview you have in mind. Is it because the
interviewee happens to live in your town? To satisfy your
long-held hankering to talk to your favourite pop-star? Your
kid brother would love a signed photograph of the First
Division footballer? You might get a free trip to Spain to interview a leading film star? None of these reasons is adequate.
There is only one valid question to ask yourself: will *readers*
be interested? If the unbiased answer to this question is 'yes'
then ask yourself *why*. Will what the interview reveals give
them help with a personal problem, perhaps, or encourage
them to keep going in a difficult situation? Will they learn
something practical, gain confidence, experiment with a craft,
be safer drivers or understand the previously inexplicable?
There are many reasons why readers like a published interview: provide yourself with the answer to *why* and you will
have a strong indication of how to build its substance.

Well, I never actually met . . .

Most readers assume an interview is the result of a live
face-to-face meeting between the two people involved but

sometimes it may only be possible to conduct an interview by mail, by telephone, or with a mixture of the two. While some professional interviewers scorn mail and telephone interviews, claiming the published results clearly lack the sparkle of 'live' ones, there may be a place on some occasions, for some reasons, and in some magazines, for interviews where the participants never meet. Do not discount 'distant' interviewing, therefore, but be careful not to fall back on it too easily and remember that warning about the possible 'lack of sparkle' that may result. Aware of this you will understand that there can be something (almost) irreplaceable about talking to someone face to face which leaves telephone interviews out in the cold. In our literature, conversations by letter may reveal invaluable insights into their writers but the essence of an interview is its immediacy: its impact for magazine readers is that *they*, not you, were talking to and meeting the interviewee. A 'real' meeting may be the only way you can get a direct quote, hear your interviewee's voice – and perhaps its undertones revealing what he *didn't* say – and feel his friendliness. If you never met him it will be harder to let readers share these emotions.

If your interviewee lives hundreds of miles away or in another country and there is no chance of your going to see him you may have no alternative but to do the job by mail or phone. For the former a carefully worded list of questions can produce the best results. (Be sure to include an adequately stamped addressed envelope to make it easy for him to reply.) To interview him by telephone it is best to arrange, by post, the date and time of your call – to suit him, of course – and to have a questionnaire of your own prepared.

On the few occasions when I've had to interview someone by phone I've found myself wandering from my prepared list of questions as the moment throws up more pertinent ones. As this is likely to happen to your advantage (and the interview's) make sure you record the phone conversation *if you have your interviewee's permission to do so*. Some folk are uneasy knowing your electronic device is recording everything they say and if your interviewee is one of these you'll have to rely on your own handwriting. With practice your note-taking ability will improve but be careful to make it legible at all times. Not being able to read your own writing is always galling. Interview notes you can't decipher are particularly frustrating and may negate the whole enterprise. *You only have one chance to make them.* With the sophistication of modern recording equipment 'old-fashioned' shorthand is becoming a lost skill but I can't over-emphasise its value. Tape-recorders have their uses, but they can never replace shorthand in every situation.

The initial approach

So, who's going to be lucky? Where is this potential interviewee waiting for you to come along and write his story to dazzle editors and set the magazine pages on fire? There is no room for on-spec or seizing-the-opportunity interviews in magazine work as the pace of production of even the most frequently published allows time to make all necessary arrangements and complete the work preceding publication.

In truth, the necessary preamble to interviewing is usually downbeat, even humdrum. It demands study and research as dedicated as for any other type of writing. Someone in the public eye now may not be worth reading about when the magazine you are writing for is published, so the first factor to bear in mind is *topicality*. Consider the time-schedules discussed in Chapter 2 and discard anyone who may not be 'in vogue' in, say, two months' time. And even 'famous' people may have exhausted their special cachet by the time your interview would be published.

An unknown person might have a personal story that would make ideal material. So could someone revealing an achievement of particular interest to readers of your targeted magazine. As writing for a market is merely giving readers what they want, the choice of a person to interview is simply giving readers the person they want. Fortunately, for writers, the world is full of 'ordinary' people. Many of them are caught up in events so dramatic, so thrilling, so tragic, so inspiring, so unbelievable or in some way so unusual that finding interviewees is not hard. Even though you will not sound out those already well interviewed elsewhere or only available a costly distance away or likely to scorn your approach (although you can't be sure ...) or known to demand a fee for allowing you access (never, under any circumstances, agree to pay an interviewee for the so-called 'privilege' of interviewing him), there are still more than enough folk each with a different story to tell and an individual experience in life.

Thinking of or discovering interviewees is itself an exciting spur to the job ahead. Choices made, and armed with a list of several people, the next step is . . .

Getting editors interested

In the sequence of events leading to the interview, when is the best time to talk to editors and sell the idea? This may depend on how well you know the editor you have in mind and how well he knows you. From your experience of him, his likes, dislikes and favoured way of working, only you can decide which comes first: querying the editor about an interview with Mr X, or suggesting the same thing to Mr X while not yet being able to promise him it will be published. The chicken-or-egg matter is likely to be resolved without trouble if your work is already known to the editor and he can rely on your not suggesting an interview with someone unsuitable. Your friendly editor could invite you to go ahead, probably without any obligation on his part but perhaps with encouraging noises. He will certainly tell you if the idea is a non-starter, and if that is the case there may be no poor reflection on you or your abilities. The editor may know, as you can't, that he or a rival editor already has an interview with Mr X in the pipeline or that Mr X has refused to be interviewed for his magazine in the past. Mr X may, unknown to you, be considered more trouble than he is worth, demanding apologies and causing endless correspondence and aggravation.

A helpful editor may offer you suggestions about interviewees he would like to feature in his pages, but regardless of who originates the idea, if he is confident you can do the job he is likely to offer you a commission, i.e. a definite 'Yes, go ahead'. One important point to remember here: even being given a commission (and it makes no difference whether it is in writing or merely verbal, although you may feel happier with the former) even a 'definite commission' is subject to the editor's evaluation of the finished article. If the work's not good enough, cries of 'But you promised . . .' will fall on deaf ears. (See Kill fees in Chapter 12 for the legal position on this point.)

Supposing you have no previous contact with your chosen magazine and are going in 'cold'? In this case it is better to establish contact with your potential interviewee, albeit having to explain to him that you do not at this stage know where or even if you are going to sell the piece. While this is not the most flattering approach (and one guaranteed to offend well-known figures) it is most unlikely you will find a magazine editor commissioning an interview conducted by someone whose work is totally unknown to him. At best you might get a loose 'We don't mind having a look but can't promise . . .' which is not an entirely satisfactory basis for the whole enterprise.

Whatever your relationship or non-relationship with the editor of your choice, the selling of the interview is important to the job itself, even if it exists only in your pipe dreams at the time. When you can tell a potential interviewee you have a commission to interview him for XYZ magazine his response is likely to be far more positive.

This point emphasises three aspects of interviewing:

1 Editors only commission writers whose work they know they can rely on.
2 To get to the above stage may take many sales and a long time.
3 Interviewing for magazines is not for beginners.

Opinions not facts

This type of writing job has one facet contrary to all you may have learned so far about mixing opinion with statements of fact. 'Readers don't want your views!' we are constantly reminded in the general course of article-writing – but readers *do* want to hear the opinions of someone sufficiently fascinating to be interviewed for the pages of a magazine. The degree of opinion you quote will depend on the interviewee in question, of course, so you will have to judge how much of what he says is relevant to the background of the interview, i.e. why he was worthy of an interview in the first place, and how much the readers will want to hear. For example, the opinion of a local councillor talking about forthcoming cuts in the town's bus service may persuade you to devote a high proportion of the interview to his justification or rebuttal of the scheme, while an interview with a young mother taking her baby to Switzerland for a rare operation might carry more opinions from medical authorities and specialists than from the mother herself. If the idea that opinions are wanted in interviews is new to you, remember one essential adjunct: the opinions must not be *yours*.

Time and place

There are other reasons why it may be auspicious to contact your potential interviewee before making definite arrangements either with him or an editor. He might decline unless you can show some evidence of having done some of your homework when you first approach him, it could be difficult for an interview to be fitted into his hectic life, or he may insist on talking to you only in particular circumstances you cannot meet without problems. It is worth remembering some folk will be deterred by the word 'interview' but might agree quite happily to 'talk' to you: choose your words carefully while making sure you don't make any promises (about privacy, etc.) you will not be able to keep.

If you haven't already approached your interviewee you will need his consent to the project. Initial contact is best by phone (to his secretary or agent, perhaps, if not directly to him) but, if you feel safer with written confirmation of all arrangements, be prepared for the 'fixing' process to take longer and remember the topicality or purpose of the interview may suffer from such delay. Sometimes less well-known interviewees want to help with research in their own interests and this may be of benefit to you as long as they understand you are under no obligation to feature any particular aspect of their work or lives.

Explain who you are, which magazine will be publishing your interview, or you hope will be publishing it, if you have not yet reached any editorial agreement, why you want to talk to him, about what, and indicate that you will readily fit in with his plans concerning dates, times, the use of a tape-recorder, the length of the interview and anything else to suit him.

If he says 'No' you'll have to decide whether he will give in if you're more persistent, whether he's learned to be wary of magazine interviews or if he truly does not want the publicity a published interview will provide. Many newspaper interviewers are ruthless, pursuing reluctant victims, heedless of their wishes or protests: the results are frequently a source of complaints against journalists and newspaper editors. Because the pace of magazines is gentler don't imagine the business is any less tough in the commercial sense: money has to be made, circulation has to be maintained and preferably increased, and readers have to be satisfied. But on the whole interviews in magazines are arranged, given and published to the satisfaction of everyone concerned.

Where and when should the interview take place? If you are in a position to choose remember an interview over a meal is seldom wise. Balancing plates, pens, notebooks, eating, drinking, asking questions and recording answers all at the same time is not easy. Nor is it always a good idea to meet at your interviewee's home, although agreeing to such an invitation could make him feel more at ease than he might be elsewhere. Suggesting a venue where the interview is unlikely to be disrupted by outside influences such as children, animals and general interruptions is more sensible; and could be the first test of your tact and discretion.

Groundwork

In any published interview some of the questions put by the interviewer may be just what you would have liked to ask if you had been doing the job. They flow with the natural informality of spontaneous conversation, giving readers a warm impression of being *there*. Writers aren't fooled. Questions that appear impromptu have been carefully planned and are cunningly inserted at the most appropriate moments. Background details of the interviewee's life, for example, may be mentioned casually but have been checked scrupulously long before the interview takes place.

Preparing the ground is part of most non-fiction work; certainly no magazine interview could succeed without it. Only later, at the interview itself, will the time and effort devoted to your groundwork prove its value. And here's an agreeable surprise: groundwork is engrossing. The facts about a celebrity's childhood, the early problems an 'ordinary' person overcame with extraordinary braveness or the details of a potential interviewee's lifestyle and habits could prove so interesting you may fear conducting the interview itself will be a disappointment by comparison. Don't worry: there is no rule that states preparation must be a chore, and if you find you enjoy it so much the better. You can be sure the more thoroughly it is done the more pleasant will be the interview that follows.

It is important to discover all you can about your interviewee so you don't waste time at the interview asking him questions you could well have found the answers to before you met. You will have confidence when you meet him if you already know about his early life, his family, his career, what he does in his spare time, what his hobbies are – in fact anything and everything that might be relevant (and probably quite a lot that may not be). Not only will such prior knowledge help you, it will also please him to realise you have taken the trouble to do your groundwork before the interview. Nothing irks an interviewee more than being asked questions like 'Where were you born?' or 'What is the name of your company?'

How to find the facts (for any purpose) is discussed in Chapter 5 and much of the basic background about well-known people will be found in general reference material although there are other sources of information. Colleagues working in the same field or friends sharing your interviewee's hobbies may be able to give you help not published in any book. They may also smooth your path with, for example, any special vocabulary or knowledge you will need to be familiar with when talking to him. This can be invaluable, as I've found several times when about to interview people whose way of life or work has been totally foreign to me. Visiting a bakery before interviewing a local master baker gave me an insight, albeit a brief one, into how the work was done and helped me understand what the master baker was talking about at the time of the interview. On another occasion taking a trolley of library books round the wards in a large hospital taught me something of the value patients attach to the work of voluntary helpers. When this aspect of welfare arose during a subsequent interview with the boss of the hospital management committee I was better equipped to deal with it than I might otherwise have been. Another time a short outline from a Paraguayan acquaintance about the current history of his country put me in the picture to interview a Paraguayan diplomat who had fled to England and to understand why he was seeking refuge here. I also learned the names and aims of the warring factions in the coup he and his family were escaping from. So never miss the chance to gain some idea of the words or phrases your interviewee is likely to use and you won't have to keep asking him to explain what he means – which can be an irritant and inevitably impedes the flow of the interview.

Material already published will be useful but check it carefully; what may have been pertinent then may not be so now. Press releases, if appropriate, soon age and become valueless, and beware of any published items you find that do not bear the date of publication; they are, I suspect, just waiting for the unwary to come along and use them. They frequently spell trouble.

Collect everything together. If you find in due course you have gathered more information than you need remember it is better to have too much than too little. Later, as your experience grows, you will become more selective in your research. However well-experienced an interviewer you may become, taking pains to get the 'feel' of the interviewee before meeting him will help you judge the best way of using the material you've collected.

Writing your private guidelines

Shaping your material into order is not difficult if you've assembled plenty of notes – but before you begin you might want to refresh your mind about the format favoured by your intended market in interviews already published. This, after all, is the most important aspect of an interviewer's job – to satisfy readers. That done, decide the rough shape you'd like the interview to take. At this stage flexibility is important; setting yourself and the interviewee a programme that subsequently proves too rigid, predictable or boring will almost certainly read as rigid, predictable or boring when you come to write it up. So establish your guidelines but be prepared to depart from them.

In my early days of interviewing I kept in mind a sight I watch from the window over my desk. My cat climbs his favourite tree, often in a wild rush that takes him higher up the trunk than he intends to go, and then ventures out on to a side branch. A little way along he turns round, returns to the trunk and starts off along another branch lower down. He ventures along many branches of the tree, always returning to the central trunk before setting off again. And here's what impresses me: even when he has explored all the branches he wants to visit and could quite easily jump from the lowest to the ground he goes back to the trunk to make his final descent. It is a perfect example of always returning to the central theme, the trunk, and of rounding off an interview, or any writing job, by making a neat exit appropriate to where you began. And he's only a cat! (I think he might be a reincarnated writer.)

An interview is not just a question-and-answer session. 'What would I like to know about him?' is a good question to ask yourself. You might plan your questions chronologically beginning with your interviewee's childhood and family life, continuing with how his career began, his problems, achievements and so on, according to what is suitable to his story. But interviews conducted this way often drag even if they get off the ground at all. Opening with a reader-grabbing sentence or question, like my cat's dramatic dash up the tree, is as important in interviewing as it is in any other type of writing. Available space may also preclude telling the interviewee's entire story. Your decision about where to start will be determined by what your market wants and, above all, whatever it is that makes your interviewee of special interest to readers at that time. Your thoughts on how to plan the questions to ask must be tempered by these considerations.

Just as some computer software programs aim to help you sort out the planning of any article, others are designed to ease the pattern of interview questions and answers. Despite this particular technological aid I generally begin with paper and pencil, writing down key questions as they occur to me on a large sheet of paper, leaving plenty of space between items so I have room for adding subsidiary questions. This way I can change my mind about where to start and what to ask at any particular point in the interview. There is often a great deal of reorganising and inserting new ideas before I am temporarily satisfied with my outline plan.

Computer users may like to try an electronic method of planning how an interview might proceed. Such programs are not hard to use and can make short work of the business of getting your questions straight. One to try is:

Brainstorm. Brainstorm Software Limited, 18 Courtlands Close, Ruislip, Middlesex HA4 8AX. Tel: 0895 677845. This is an effective ideas-processor that was developed specifically to provide its creator with 'a place to store, explore, structure and modify all my thoughts, information and actions. I was aiming for a clear head.' Once you have entered your data (which is simply done) it can certainly prove useful in letting you choose how to design your interview, for instance, how to avoid repeating questions and how to extract only what you need from your collected material. £50 or less according to your machine.

It is wise to keep opening questions general rather than specific and not to plunge into anything likely to be controversial or provoke your interviewee to apprehension or hostility. Questions that vary in length and depth are most easily answered but avoid those requiring only a 'yes' or 'no' response. Indicate your genuine interest with thoughtful and sympathetic questioning and your interviewee will be encouraged to expand on his replies with greater relaxation and warmth, speaking more freely and informally. Ideally, to the innocent reader, an interview should seem to be a spontaneous conversation.

You may find, perhaps to your surprise, that you have a formidable amount of information about your interviewee, especially if he is well known. How can you handle all these notes during the interview? This is when you must choose what aspects of his life or work you can skate over or leave out altogether. Maybe he is a fine amateur cook or a keen rock-climber: if you are interviewing him for, let us say, his fame as a brilliant tenor you may decide not to refer to either the cooking or rock-climbing. But dropping such intriguing snippets into the conversation can lend it extra interest so you might bear these other activities in the back of your mind (with single word reminders in your guidelines such as 'cook' or 'rocks'), ready to bring them to the fore if the moment seems propitious.

Preparing the notes I'm going to take with me, I leave plenty of space after each question for the interviewee's reply if I'm relying on my own shorthand or notes. A second sheet of questions behind the first will carry subsidiary questions and reminders of anything I might forget as well as quick *aides-mémoire* to the basic statistics about my interviewee. Even if this back-up sheet is not consulted or looked at again, merely knowing it is there is a great boost to my confidence. If you plan to use a portable recorder make sure it is reliable, that you are very familiar with how it works and that the tape is of adequate length. And if you will have to reload during the interview, practise until you can do so swiftly and without fuss. There are several good models available, not all are expensive or difficult to operate and using one will free you from having to take your eyes from your interviewee and his surroundings.

Face to face

Remember to take everything you're going to need for the interview (including your watch) and arrive promptly; for an interviewer who wants to set a cool, calm and collected scene that means getting to the appointed place before the arranged time. Bring your equipment out casually during friendly talk before the interview begins. You may also like to confirm how long he expects the interview will last. Do you feel more comfortable with your watch on the table or on your wrist? Checking the time too obviously may be annoying for both of you. Also consider whether you want your notebook on your lap or on a table. It's on my lap almost every time so I can hold it up if I like and don't have to lift and lower my head to consult and take notes (I can also keep him in the corner of my eye when he thinks I'm not looking at him). Maintaining good eye contact with your interviewee is likely to make the conversation flow smoothly and there will be less jerkiness between your questions and his answers.

If daylight is likely to fade before the interview is over will you still be able to see him and your notes? Will he be able to hear you distinctly (might he be a little deaf?) and will you hear his answers clearly? How much small talk should you indulge in at your meeting? It's natural to be a little nervous, particularly if you've never met your interviewee before; some interviewers, like some actors, claim it keeps the adrenalin flowing and is more of a help than a hindrance. Your man (or woman) may have more interview experience than you have and may even take advantage of your nervousness. Fear not. If he seems superior or semi-hostile in your first moments together be careful not to react in the same manner. You are not meeting him as a 'friend', although ideally your interview will be on friendly terms and you may emerge from it with a real liking for him, but as a job. This may sound cold and calculating but it must be foremost in your mind: *you want something out of him*. Happily there is often a softening of any opening danger signals as the interview progresses and you both get into your stride. I recall several instances where my first feelings proved wholly mistaken and can truly say . I have never conducted a magazine interview I have not thoroughly enjoyed. These points about lighting, hearing and initial impressions are generally resolved instinctively without any trouble when you settle down. Now it's time to begin . . .

After the first few moments you will find you've forgotten any initial nervousness; this is the time for concentration. As you ask your questions and take note of his replies (if you are not recording them), don't be so keen to have your next question ready that you don't really listen to what he's saying. Even with a recorder, you are taking part in a two-way conversation and how that goes will determine the way in which you ask your questions. Your attitude will affect the interview and his may be particularly revealing. Crossing the knees towards another person is, I'm told by experts, a sign of being at ease with him. Does your interviewee feel at ease with you? If you're inserting questions you've only thought of when the interview is in full swing, so much the better. And don't be afraid of acknowledging a mistake if you make one: such sincerity will elicit greater relaxation and more spontaneous replies to your questions.

Maintaining the tone of the interview is all important. Needle your interviewee and he may stay silent. Irritate him and you could be shown the door. If you have established a certain rapport you may be able to ask a 'risky' question, perhaps as if you've only just thought of it, that might give you some of your most valuable information. With a light touch, an understanding attitude and sympathetic judgement of his preferred pace, there is a time to keep silent in most interviews. The whole purpose, after all, is to get him to do the talking and the fewer questions you have to ask the better. Just a nod or a smile may be appropriate at times and a little break may be useful for both of you. While he or somebody else organises a cup of tea you will be catching up on your next question and any notes you've taken so far.

Oh dear

Interviewing is a satisfying job but just occasionally it can go wrong. If you have prepared the ground thoroughly this is not likely to happen, but the most likely problem could concern what your interviewee does or does not want you to write – accompanied by coercion, bribes, warnings or even threats. Fortunately such rare occurrences are easy to deal with; you simply walk out as politely as you can in the circumstances. You will, of course, have to tell your editor you cannot proceed and there will be no published interview.

Interviewing is immensely enjoyable and often surprising. You may think you have it all resolved and that everything has gone as you planned it would and then – wham! He drops a bomb-shell: he's left his wife, he's emigrating – or whatever, in his context, is dramatic news. When that happens you have a news story that can't wait for an interview in a magazine to be printed a few weeks or even months hence. You have an item for a newspaper – but that's another story.

Writing it up

I advise writing it up as soon as you can, thereby lessening the risk of thinking something was said when it wasn't. It's wise to set down on paper as soon as you possibly can any specially valuable parting comments he made that you couldn't record and have been nourishing in your head all the way home. If you've done your market study well you know you have to catch your readers' attention at the very start.

Your task is to make them feel *they* had been talking to your interviewee, not you. Perhaps he said something that made you laugh? Did anything give you a jolt or intrigue you? If it did, it will do the same for readers. Once launched on the job of writing it up you can deftly set the scene of where the interview took place to help readers picture it. They want to know about people, with only enough background of their houses and families to help establish an image, so don't labour the point. It is better to drop such information in gradually and almost casually so it may be absorbed by readers without their being aware of what they are taking in.

The less of 'you' in the interview the better and your market will probably indicate just how much you appear at all. As a friend telling readers how you went to interview Mr X and what you found? Or does your editor favour an unadorned Question and Answer format? Are you writing your questions in direct speech ('What has given you the most pleasure in life?') or reported speech ('I asked what had given him the most pleasure in life')? The former brings interviews alive but a balance of the two gives them a natural feeling. Only you can judge the best tone for your written interview but guard against flippancy even if your interviewee and the purpose of the interview are in the 'jokey and fun' category. Toss it off too lightly, with the best of intentions, and you may lose your readers' confidence.

Filing

The task is finished. 'Filing', in professional parlance, simply means sending or taking it to your chosen magazine. But wait: there may still be one or two points to attend to.

Don't forget to enclose any pictures you might have offered the editor to go with your interview. And send a stamped self-addressed envelope unless you are certain he won't feel a pang of irritation when he doesn't find one. After so much work and effort on your part it would be a shame to risk spoiling your chances for the sake of a postage stamp.

One thing leads to another . . .

When an interview is eventually published there is one further minor job to be done. Send a copy of the magazine carrying it to your interviewee, even though you think he may have seen it already, with a brief 'Thank you' note. He'll be pleased at this small courtesy but there is more than politeness behind this simple gesture. If his friends or working colleagues are equally good interview material, you may find one working assignment you thoroughly enjoyed can lead to another . . .

9
Is this your problem?

'I'm in the habit of writing a great deal and then cutting a lot of it out for a "tighter" way of writing. I feel I must have plenty to chop at in order to get the best results but this does seem a waste of time and effort. Any suggestions?'

It does seem wasteful to write too much and then throw away some of what you've written. It's a pity we writers don't have a built-in editing ability that works without thought when we are in the process of writing. Words do not come to order and phrases, the ones we know will be ideal for that very point, are annoyingly out of the mind's reach. Word-processors offer a tempting solution: get it all down higgledy-piggledy and tidy it up later. Hmm. George Bernard Shaw wrote a very long letter to a friend, ending with this apology: 'Sorry, but I did not have time to write a short letter.' We know what he meant. But don't be too hard on yourself. In an ideal world there would be no editing at all, for everyone, including you, would write the ideal copy straight on to the paper at the first touch of the keyboard.

There is a section on editing your own work at the end of Chapter 4 which you should read with care – and determination to be better organised in the way you write.

'I feel I will never make a success of writing because I have not had a good education and I don't know the right words to use.'

Forget any idea that high-sounding words and convoluted phrases are the signs of 'good' writing. The very reverse is true. Clear and concise English is always preferable to literary verbosity and using obscure words in the expectation of attracting readers generally has quite the opposite effect: they turn away in droves, unimpressed, irritated or just plain bored. Don't be discouraged by what you call lack of a 'good education'. Many leading writers and hundreds of lesser-known ones missed out on normal let alone extended education. One top-rank novelist once told me she was *glad* she didn't understand syntax or feel happy using long words. 'I just write from the heart' she said, 'and readers understand because their hearts feel the same as mine. We don't need high-sounding language.'

'Without proper training, won't I always be classed as an amateur?'

This naturally follows the question above but there is more in Chapter 12 about official training in journalism. Such training can be helpful (it gave me many advantages at the start of my career) but I have found that more than half the men and women working on the staff of UK newspapers and magazines received no official training whatever. In the freelance world the proportion of officially 'untrained' writers must be a great deal higher so you are in good company: the best, in fact. I'll guarantee most of the top well-known freelance writers are, in a sense, as 'amateur' as you are. So what is the difference between them and you? Just this: the state of being an amateur lies not in your qualifications but in *your working attitude.* Ignore market study, despise research and be a trial to editors everywhere and you will always be an amateur, even if you've been doing it for years: but take a *professional* view of the worthwhile task you set yourself, follow the advice in this book and others – and nobody will have any reason to be derogatory about your status as a writer.

'Is it all right to send hand-written work while my word-processor is out of action?'

No – unless you are writing for the 'Letters to the Editor' section of a magazine where *legible* hand-writing is normally acceptable. (Some folk think it is even *preferable*, giving a more personal and less 'professional-writer' impression.) This exception apart, excuses about your equipment being repaired, a finger being broken or even your electricity supply being cut off render your copy totally unacceptable. It won't be accepted because it won't even be read! If this sounds hard – well, the truth is that magazine staff cannot spend time trying to decipher hand-written copy (which may seem clearly written to the writer but is often less so to the reader) when there is probably a pile of neatly presented easy-to-read work awaiting attention and possible acceptance. The solution? If you can't beg, borrow or hire a machine, fill in the time with market study, research, straightening out your business affairs and clearing your desk until your word-processor is returned in working order.

'How many words a day is considered reasonable?'

How much ink is there in your pen or how long will your fingers type for before they drop off? In the course of straight writing, i.e. letting it flow out of your head without having to pause to consult reference books, outline structure plans or notes of any kind, what is 'reasonable' to you will probably only be determined by the hours at your disposal and your level of fatigue. One well-published writer I know averages at least 1000 words a day in straight writing while another, equally well-established, seldom manages more than 200.

Work on a project where you have to keep stopping for the reasons above and inevitably the number of words produced in any given time falls. But don't worry if you don't write a huge amount every day. Far more valuable is the habit of writing *something* regularly, preferably daily. Remember, too, that time spent in planning, researching and all the other writing 'chores' is productive time, even though you may not have a great many words on paper to show for it. Most important of all, of course, is that the words you write, even if they only total 50 or 100, are the right ones!

'Would it be a good idea to make my own rejection slips? It might save editors time.'

If you're joking you might make editors laugh as they automatically reject your copy. If you're serious – but, no, I can't believe any writer would be so bent on self-destruction. A few writers enclose with their copy a simple type of questionnaire for editors to complete: tick as applicable – unwanted topic, unsuitable treatment, insufficiently researched and so on, but many editors dislike this and feel (rightly, in my opinion) that the onus of spotting what is wrong with copy is on writers before they submit it .

'I suffer from writer's rush, finding it hard to concentrate on just one writing project at one time. Is this a mistake?'

If it is, I share your faults. But long ago I decided to stop fighting what must be a natural instinct and make use of it instead.

So now I relish the business of writing two or three – or more – pieces of work during the same period. Initially I told myself that each changeover time would let me bring a fresh look and renewed zeal to all the projects in hand and one day I realised that was exactly what was happening. So if this is the way you like working, *and it works*, why alter it? Please note those little words *and it works* because they are all important. But if dodging from one piece of work to the next leaves none of them completed – that really *is* a mistake.

'Sometimes in the middle of a piece that's going well I dry up completely. If this is the dreaded "writer's block" how do I overcome it?'

I used to think I was just lucky never to suffer from writer's block until I realised it was impossible to have block and rush (as in the previous question) at the same time. That, I'm sure, is the answer: give yourself so much writing to do, preferably of different sorts, that you defeat any threatening block with a neat bit of attention-switching to one of your other tasks. The multi-tasking capabilities of my computer make this a doddle. It's easy to attend to correspondence, write copy, keep research up to date, make decisions about which pix to use, update records and half a dozen other duties just with the press of a key. With so much on hand at once (if I want it) writer's block can't get a word in. The answer must be, therefore, have plenty to do and when the block lurks – turn to something else.

'How do I know a magazine is not going to reject my article, steal my idea and rehash it for themselves, so avoiding the need to pay me?'

You don't. But it's very unlikely such a thing will occur. In any case what you fear is technically impossible as there is no copyright in *ideas*. The worst that could happen is that somebody else writes another article based on your idea or something like it. The new article would not be a copy of yours for, had yours been good enough in the first place, it would have been accepted for publication.

'I write quickly and am at my best when in full flow but come to a halt when I need information about a point I haven't yet researched. For instance, I might want to insert facts or figures to

develop my theme but if I have to stop and look something up all impetus is lost. How can I avoid this break when the writing is going so well?'

Here's a useful word-processing tip for just such times: I call it my 'OOO accelerator' because far from making me pause it speeds up the process of writing. Let three Os – OOO – indicate a spot where you know more work must be done (perhaps a fact to be checked or some further research to be completed) when you don't want to stop to do it as you write. Not having to pause lets you write more easily than you might otherwise do and the comfort of knowing you can quickly find where you want to insert something in due course means there is no 'I must remember to put X in there' niggling in your mind as you're working. This is especially handy if you write straight on to a word-processor, as most writers now do, for the simplest 'Find' command will immediately locate your 'Os' when you are ready to fill the spaces they have reserved for you. My machine happily inserts other special markers in the text wherever I want it to, as yours may, but I still find OOO easier to use for this particular function. I chose OOO because an O indicates a hole that needs filling. The word-processor's 'Find' will never let me down as there are no English words containing a string of three Os. If you work with a typewriter the 'OOO accelerator' can still be useful, marking places in your first draft where further research is required.

'If it's possible to use the wrong word you can be sure I will do so. How can I improve my vocabulary?'

Those of us who misuse words are most likely to fall into error when we are blithely unaware of having done so. If you don't know you're making a mistake it will go uncorrected until someone tells you about it or you realise it yourself. For years I used a word I spelt as *lasvicious*. I said it too: *lass-vicious*. Folk who listened to me and read what I wrote were too kind for my own good and nobody corrected me: they just noted my ignorance in silence. Gradually it dawned on me the word was *lascivious*, a wild, wanton, licentious word, and I'd been making a fool of myself with it all this time. Do you suspect the same thing might be happening to you? Even if you are reasonably confident of your own ability (as I was) beg your close friends to correct you when you are wrong and they'll be doing you a good turn.

Do you need to know the size and extent of your vocabulary? Word-processor peripherals generally include the ability to count the number of words in a written piece and report on how frequently each word has been used. The more sophisticated suggest alternative words to use should you wish to change your first choices. Does such mechanical analysis threaten to reduce us to computer-operated robots? Shall we soon merely order up words 485, 6029, 312, and so on – and lo! there is our copy all ready? But a computer *is* only a robot. As such it makes a good servant and should *never* be allowed airs and graces, for it is certainly a poor – and often disastrous – master. As long as that is not forgotten, measuring vocabulary can be an enlightening experience from which most of us may benefit.

More people whose native tongue is not English study it as a second language than study any other. That sounds as if we whose first language is English should excel at using it; skilled carefully conducted surveys tell a different story. Although even professional lexicographers cannot say exactly how many English words exist, there are thought to be just over a million available for common use. In addition to this a further half million or so fall into the technical or specialist category. A small proportion of the reasonably intelligent and articulate adults in this country uses about 25,000–30,000 words regularly while the majority in the same category manage with about 15,000 (that's *less* than 1.5 per cent of the total). But the average person with no higher education or adult literacy skills is probably content with a vocabulary bank balance of between three and four thousand words – a pitiful proportion of what is available to everybody in any good dictionary.

Are you wondering how to count the number of words you know? There are several prescriptions, tried, tested and producing remarkably similar results. One is known as the Flesch Readability Formula which involves taking a sample of your written work, noting the average sentence length, the number of words and syllables – and risking oblivion in a mathematical morass before being presented with a result you might prefer not to know after all. Another way is to count the number of words on any page in an established English dictionary and check how many of them you already know. Do this for several different pages and it is not difficult to gain an unpolished idea of the extent of your vocabulary.

Undoubtedly the more words you know the better your powers of communication will be. With a wide knowledge of English words to choose from you can more easily express your thoughts and ideas as you wish. And communication works both ways. Not only are you, the writer, restricted by the words in your personal word-bank, readers also are imprisoned by their vocabularies – which will certainly not be the same as yours. In general our reading vocabulary is more extensive than our writing vocabulary because some of the words we read we understand but lack the confidence to use in our written work. It is up to us to expand our own store of words we hear, read and write.

For steady but sure improvement read as much as you can, listen carefully to other people and browse through dictionaries. You'll find your vocabulary improves almost without your realising it. Just to build your confidence, test yourself with these words: disaffected/unaffected, stalactite/stalagmite, billion/trillion, seasonal/seasonable, imply/infer – can you be sure of using them correctly?

'I am longing to take the plunge, throw away my old typewriter and move over to the new technology but I receive so many conflicting opinions from well-meaning friends I am confused. Some say I will never understand a computer, so which word-processor do you recommend?'

When the Research and Development Department of the British Library recently undertook a detailed investigation into the future of the communications industry, the changes in the way authors work and submit their copy to editors was one of the most significant findings. Certainly for all writers, be the end product books, magazines or newspapers, the future looks very different from the present. Persist in the old-fashioned method of presenting your work on sheets of paper, putting them in an envelope, sticking a stamp on, posting it and waiting for a response: oh no, follow that quaint outdated pattern (said the report) and you will achieve nothing. By the turn of the century (it continued) it is possible we shall all be wholly electronic – and that doesn't mean just using our word-processors or spell-checkers or word-counters or whatever clever devices so beguile us now.

For some of us this new golden age has already begun. Be attached to the right editorial office by the pertinent equipment, feed your copy into it in the appropriate format and the job is done. Work written on your home computer is electronically transferred to your editor's office either in the form of entire disks or as shorter individual pieces. Once you are set up with the gadgetry required to effect electronic filing the expense of using it is not great. In most cases transmission may take place during the cheaper off-peak hours.

If you're lost already, don't worry about how you will take to this modern style of writing and presentation. It's barely arrived yet but just imagine it: you won't need any paper for all your work will be stored on disk. Your printer or type-writer will gather dust from misuse, you needn't buy any envelopes and you'll save a fortune in stamps.

Well, that's the theory. I have worked for years on as up-to-date electronic equipment as I can afford, revelling in the help provided by all its brilliant attributes. I'm all for progress. But it doesn't always happen at the rate experts predict for it and so, if you are happy with your present working machinery, please don't let anyone's criticism or prognostications depress you.

First of all you should be clear about the difference between a word-processor, which will only process words, and a computer – which will run a word-processing program but also do many other useful tasks: keeping records in a data-base (think of that as an automatically cross-referencing filing cabinet) is just one of them. Most computers will also let you make line drawings and use pictures as part of their word-processing package – which most word-processor-only machines will not do. Which do you want? If you are sure you only need to use words, juggle them around with ease, move whole sentences and paragraphs at the touch of a couple of keys etc. *and nothing more*, you could buy a word-processor, perhaps an Amstrad PCW – although there are others equally recommended.

But think again, please. Ideally, don't waste your time on a machine that only processes words. A computer, with all its enhanced features, is more expensive but I can't advise you to buy anything less. In no time at all you'll wonder how you ever managed without its many extra facilities.

The choice between Amiga, DOS (IBM-compatible), Macintosh and other lesser-known machines is often a matter of which you grew up with or were introduced to by friends. DOS, incidentally, simply stands for disk-operating system.

Not wishing to start any battles I can only recommend my own choice and that of most of my colleagues (which is not necessarily the same thing). My Amiga is my first love and does all I want, including everything all the others mentioned here also do – and does most of them better – while they do not do all the Amiga does. But the majority of writers do not agree with me. DOS machines are the most popular, many of them using an operating environment called 'Windows' and there is no doubt that this popular PC format (PC simply means Personal Computer) is most widely used.

As for the specific word-processor to use with your new computer – that will depend on its type and capacity. For the DOS (and, in many cases 'Windows') families three word-processors are the big sellers and there is little to choose between them. Some folk prefer one, some the other:

WordPerfect, Wordperfect United Kingdom, Weybridge Business Park, Addlestone Road, Addlestone, Surrey KY15 2UU. Tel: 0932 850505. Relatively easy to learn (considering its many complex facilities) and used in the offices of many magazines, this is the industry standard in word-processing technology. It is packed with features to make your writing flow smoothly and your editing a pleasure rather than a chore.

Wordstar, Wordstar International Limited, Chancery House, St Nicholas Way, Sutton, Surrey SM1 1JB. Tel: 081-643 8866. A supreme combination of text-handling features. Like other leading software it takes a while to understand. But it is well worth learning and can transform your writing method from one of constant rewriting to total control of structure, paragraphing, paginating, style and many other features. Enthusiastic touch-typists claim they control the whole program without ever lifting their fingers from the keys.

Protext, Arnor Ltd, 611 Lincoln Road, Peterborough PE1 3HA. Tel: 0733 68909. A brilliant program with many outstanding features too numerous to mention here. Many writers swear 'once used, never forsaken'. Not hard to learn, *fast*, a joy to use and fully compatible with a variety of databases and spreadsheets, *Protext* is my personal favourite. It has been used to write this book.

To understand just what DOS is and how to make the very best use of its power for your own customised benefit, read:

DOS by Ruth Ashley and Judi N. Fernandez, John Wiley & Sons Ltd, Baffins Lane, Chichester, West Sussex PO19 1UD. Tel: 0243 779777.

In the more expensive Macintosh world I suggest **MacWrite** as quality software and for PC users needing to transfer Macintosh files directly to their DOS-based systems I highly recommend:

Mac-in-DOS for Personal Computers, Riva, 3 Industrial Centre, Bentley, Farnham, Surrey GU10 5NJ. Tel: 0420 22666.

One last point on the topic of computers. They break down. Not often but sometimes. Don't throw your old typewriter away.

'I can see my writing is flat and my writing friends tell me it is often in the wrong voice. What does this mean?'

Broadly speaking it means writing 'actively', i.e. close to the reader, or 'passively' – more at a distance. Verbs have two voices. Listen to someone telling a story (a non-fiction one as well as an invented one) in the active voice and its immediacy keeps you on your toes to know what happened next. Then hear another one told from the other side, i.e. in the passive voice, and it is, in comparison, dull and certainly not so exciting. There is less urgency and the whole thing seems further away. To make stories stand out and demand attention, write in the active voice as much as possible unless you are deliberately using the passive for special effect at any point. Using the active voice does not necessarily mean writing in the first person: rather it is telling the tale through the eyes of the person your reader is identifying with at the time – and that helps bring the story to life. Like this:

A six-year-old boy carried the baby to safety in almost pitch darkness across fifty yards of slippery rocks. (Active)

The baby was carried to safety in almost pitch darkness across fifty yards of slippery rocks by a six-year-old boy. (Passive)

'I'm in a muddle about when to use capital letters. What should I do?'

Don't groan if I tell you the obvious answer: study the market. That really is the only way to find out what the custom is in the magazine you intend to submit to. Even so there are some titles that don't seem to adhere to any particular rules or break them as often as they observe them. So the following comments apply only when you cannot, for whatever reason, discover the relevant house style on capital letters.

Doubt about whether or not to start a particular word with a capital letter may bring writing that is flowing well to an unwelcome halt. A few principles are worth remembering. Capitals, incidentally, are known in the trade as *upper case*, a term inherited by modern technology from the top half of the old compositors' type cases in which capital letters, reference marks and accents were kept. Other letters we tend to think of as 'ordinary' were, and still are, referred to as *lower case*. Upper-case letters are normally used in written English for the following:

- At the beginning of sentences and quotations and following a point (which you may prefer to call a *full stop* or *period*): 'I am going out,' he said, 'and may not return.' (Note the second half of the sentence begins in lower case because it follows a comma, not a point.)
- Proper names, modes of address and special titles: John Smith, Trafalgar Square, Africa, Tuesday, Mrs Jones, Lord Brown, His Royal Highness, Chief Constable, Member of Parliament.
- Titles of magazines, books, plays, etc.: Good Housekeeping, Jamaica Inn, Doctor Faustus.
- Religious events and organisations: Christmas, Lent, Church of England.
- Single-letter words and exclamations: I, Oh!
- Acronyms (words formed from or based on the initial letters of titles or official bodies): JP, RAF, UN. It is worth observing that most initials in sets now thrive without the points that used to separate them. Even the full stop that was once customary after Mr. or Mrs. has decayed and dropped out of sight.

Don't you laugh at sentences like this that we occasionally find?

'The director of TR will attend the EDC today in an attempt to add MH and GNJ to next month's agenda when delegates at the PIF conference meet in London.'

You understand exactly, I'm sure . . .

10
Presentation – going public

The writing's finished, everything's tidied up and all that remains is to send off your copy. If you've dealt with the editor or features editor you will know the person to send your work to and the correct address. But if you've only spoken to a voice on the phone at the preliminary stages (which may have been quite a while ago) or, worse still, are submitting to a magazine out of the blue, you may be unsure about how it should be addressed. Do you send an accompanying letter, and if so, what should it say? Can you ask the magazine's office to telephone you to confirm your work has arrived safely? Should you send more than one copy? How big should be the stamped self-addressed envelope you send with your copy or does sending one at all tell the recipient you are expecting it to be rejected? These and similar questions beset newcomers to writing for magazines. But the matter of presentation is, in fact, both simple and painless.

How magazines are organised

Knowing how a magazine is organised and how its office is run (or should be run, which is not always the same thing) is helpful. Just as efficient organisation in your kitchen at home differs from that necessary for the smooth running of the kitchens behind the scenes of a large international restaurant, so magazine offices differ in the way they are arranged and managed.

The size of the staff, the space in the office, the age and effectiveness of its equipment and the overall confidence of the whole set-up are ruthlessly determined by one thing: profitability. In a world of recession, as I write this book, many magazines are fighting to survive and every day some give up the struggle. It is true that the number of new titles launched continues at a high level despite the current economic gloom. But when deaths follow births at an alarming rate, when advertisers can't afford to buy as much space on magazine pages as they used to, when the buying public is having to spend less on periodicals and when costs of paper, distribution and everything else continue to rise, the air in many magazine offices is one of hanging on rather than bursting ahead.

Given this background (and there are exceptions, of course) each edition must reflect a very different view. New readers must be attracted and the old ones retained: everything must be done for the maximum impact with depleted staff and an increasingly restricted budget. How is it done?

Magazines of substantial size and those running as part of large groups are generally organised into five main departments:

1 Editorial – which is what mostly concerns writers.
2 Advertising – persuading clients to buy magazine space to advertise their wares.
3 Production – printing and handling the physical making of the magazine.
4 Sales – dealing with circulation and distribution.
5 Administration – running the office, perhaps the building as well, the secretarial side, finance, stationery, insurance and everything else that needs attending to.

All five departments cost money to run but only two, advertising and sales, produce income. In times of financial trouble even the money raised from cover prices may barely compensate for the costs of running the sales department. That leaves advertising as the only positive source of income and no magazine can last long in that unhappy situation.

Naturally there is a great deal of contact between the various departments, the more so in a small set-up where a handful of staff may do almost everything. As for the production: most magazines are printed by contract printers who may be located in a town miles from the office or even in a different part of the country.

Who does what and when

Back to the editorial side. If you have already made contact with the editor (or the features editor if that is the appropriate person to deal with for the magazine you are targeting) you have already passed the first hurdle and if your work has been definitely commissioned it will not be subject to a further decision at this stage. (See Chapter 12 for more on commissioned work, plus 'Query letters' in the same chapter for unsolicited material.)

But if you are going in 'cold' the first person likely to read your work will be the copy-taster. On smaller publications this may well be the assistant editor. He, and of course that also means 'she' as throughout this book, will make a quick assessment as to whether it is worth passing to the editor or features editor. It's possible the editor himself may be the person who reads unsolicited scripts if the staff numbers are short and that is how he prefers to handle the office management. A favourable decision – and you've moved up one important step.

A copy-taster is an experienced staff journalist who knows the requirements of the magazine like the back of his hand and can quickly recognise what is or could be made acceptable. When faced with a pile of unsolicited copy anyone making the decision about what to accept is likely to take only what is absolutely right for the magazine and throw the rest out. When something is so good it can't be ignored, why bother with the other material that needs cutting or rewriting? So make sure the copy that simply can't be put down is *yours*.

The editor of a magazine is the absolute boss of what is or is not printed on its pages and is closely involved in everything that goes on until an edition is complete and ready to hand to the printers. Some of the best editors care for their magazines as a parent loves a child: wanting it to be superior to its rivals, anxious for everyone to love it more than any other and agonising when something in its life turns out badly. Being an editor is hard work demanding much practical experience, but having a love for the job, as in many other occupations, undoubtedly pays dividends. If you meet an editor who declines to discuss amendments or improvements about what you offer, remember that the interests and needs of the magazine are his priorities.

If the magazine has a large number on the staff you may be dealt with by the features editor without direct reference to the editor. There will be consultation in editorial meetings about the contents of a particular issue where your work will be published, but that won't concern you and you will probably not need to know anything about it. Just be assured there is official approval from the editor for whatever the features editor may tell you.

Only a carefully assessed proportion of magazine space is reserved for features. Revenue-earning advertisements take precedence although some magazines in the non-commercial category don't take any. Features compete with editorial matter (that sometimes means little chats by the editor or announcements of what's coming in future issues), fiction (if any), reviews, regular columns and whatever else will appeal to readers. Pictures of all sorts, including those accompanying features, are usually dealt with separately (see the next chapter).

How can you best fit into the daily working plan of a magazine office? Well-presented work is important in making that vital first impression. Make it easy to read and to handle. Don't include a mixed bag such as a letter, some pictures, a caption sheet, a list of suggested ideas for the editor to consider in the future, a stamped self-addressed envelope, a yes/no questionnaire to be completed and returned and – horrors of horrors – more than one article crammed in a single package. Yes, there are such unappetising submissions regularly received in magazine offices and unless the person with the task of sorting them out is feeling exceptionally well disposed to humanity they will be returned unread.

But if your submitted copy is properly presented you can be sure it will be happily received, particularly by magazines who need to buy freelance copy and genuinely want your envelope to contain just what they are looking for. Once past the 'accept or reject' test it will be closely scrutinised by a sub-editor whose job is to make all freelance and staff-written copy ready to be printed.

The first task for the sub-editor is to fit your copy into the space on the page or pages allotted by the chief sub-editor. Then the sub (as sub-editors are commonly called) will correct grammar and punctuation to conform to the house style. He will also write crossheads (those mini headlines that help break up long articles and make them easier to read) and retitle the copy if he thinks it necessary. Don't take offence if the heading you gave the article is discarded; a new one may be chosen simply because yours contained more words than would fit in the allotted space or because, unknown to you, an adjacent headline clashes with your original title.

Please note it is not part of a sub-editor's task to check facts and figures in your copy. He is too busy preparing information for the printers; the size, shape and typeface required for each story, the page numbers, order, column width and everything else will be keeping him fully occupied. So the more you can do to ease his work the happier he will be. For an authoritative and scholarly book on such work you can't do better than read:

> **Copy Editing** by Judith Butcher, Cambridge University Press, The Edinburgh Building, Cambridge CB2 2RU. Tel: 0223 312393. Principally for authors of books, this volume is a classic reference guide for anyone involved in preparing text and illustrations for publication. It deals with a multitude of topics including house style and all aspects of the editorial processes involved in converting text or disk to printed page. For magazine writers the section on how to lay out and present bibliographical references accompanying articles is especially valuable. £19.95.

A sub needs the sound knowledge of the laws of libel and contempt for fear the magazine gets into trouble. He knows, and writers should remember, that libel is 'a published false statement, false accusation or malicious falsehood or misrepresentation in print, damaging to a person's reputation'. A sub is also very familiar with all the other work involved in every stage of publication and, of course, of the magazine's edition deadlines. He must see all copy is in good taste, good English, of the required length and shape while within the aim of the writer and the needs of the reader. Phew!

Helping the editor

The whole aim of submitting to a magazine is to please the readers and that means pleasing the editor. By chance I once discovered the editor of a local weekly magazine was a keen golfer (a sport about which I know nothing) so I sent him a piece about the early life of a well-known golfer who spent his formative years in the area. Good luck? Yes, but more a case of cashing in on it. You can do the same. Has the editor you're aiming at a published record of earlier posts held in the magazine or newspaper world? Has he any particular likes or dislikes? He'll certainly have the interests of his magazine at heart, as we've said above, and when he sees copy about something that particularly appeals to him he may find himself instinctively softening . . .

Close study of the market reveals what an editor likes but keep your eyes and ears open for sudden editorial changes. Editor A might favour the type of story you have been at pains to research and write but before you have time to submit it has gone and editor B has taken over. What do you do? First of all find out whether editor B is of the same mind as his predecessor. He is unlikely to be so because the fact that the old editor was (perhaps) sacked indicates the magazine management were not happy about the way he was running it. Up to a point the new man will have to keep within the confines of established editorial policy, particularly if the magazine is part of a large publishing house, but new brooms can seldom resist sweeping clean.

If you are unsuccessful with editor B discover where editor A has gone. I've found the best way to do this is the simplest: ring up the office and ask whoever answers on the switchboard. If editor A has taken over another magazine which is at all suitable for what you have written and you're prepared to make whatever alterations are necessary, you could be back in business after all.

Helping yourself

If you've read of writers submitting hand-written work to editors with passages crossed out, crude insertions at the side of the text, arrows pointing to intended positions of whole paragraphs and the like, allow yourself a fond smile but *don't do the same*. Time was when such practices may have been acceptable but those times are long gone. To give your work the maximum chance of being favourably received nowadays, it is important, not to say essential, to see it is properly presented.

There's no doubt typing skill is an invaluable bonus for writers. Learning to type has proved its worth to me many times over: typing is fast and easy at the rough draft stage and with the simple editing facilities offered by good word-processing software final copy can be produced at speed. Best of all, with the eyes not on the keyboard, a touch typist can edit work on the screen without effort and that is also a time saver. If you use a word processor but cannot yet type well, why not try one of the software programs designed to teach you touch-typing? It may require patience to learn but you'll always be glad you did.

Here are a few tips from a recent study of what editors like and how unsolicited freelance submissions are received in their offices. Please note that word *recent*: old books telling you how things used to be done often recommend time-hallowed but now out-dated practices more likely to produce editorial sighs than smiles.

- Never use the word 'page' when identifying sheets of paper your copy is written on. To magazine staff the word 'page' refers to the page of the magazine as it will eventually be printed. So anything bearing the legend 'page 2', for instance, refers to page 2 of the magazine. If a sheet of your copy becomes detached and is found with 'page 2' at the top, it may be assumed to be copy marked up to appear on page 2 of the edition being prepared at the time – which may not be what the editor has in mind at all. To avoid such mistakes refer to sheets of your copy with the word 'folio', i.e. 'folio 2' not 'page 2'.

- Discover the width of a publication's standard typesetting and make your copy observe the same width. If you both work, for instance, in 9pt Garamond over 15 picas (a pica is a measurement of type size), making about 45 characters per line, the space your copy will need is quickly and easily estimated.

- Send *two* copies of your article. The second should be clearly marked DUPLICATE on every folio so it causes no confusion. It will be plainly seen to be a duplicate copy if printed on coloured paper. It may never be used or referred to but could be invaluable if any queries arise. (You will, of course, always keep a copy for yourself as well.)

- Never send more than one item of copy in a single envelope.

- Always send a stamped addressed envelope, of course, but not always one large enough for your copy's return, particularly if it is short; enclose a letter-size envelope instead. Finding a ready-to-return envelope in his hand may tempt a busy editor to shove your copy in it and wing it back to you without further thought. But if your work is left lying around the office it may be picked up

again at some less fraught time and receive more considered (and favourable) treatment. Why do you want it
back, anyway? If you have to submit it elsewhere it will
be better to present a new clean copy to another market.

Headed paper

You've finished editing your article (yes, there has to be a time
when you tell yourself enough is enough) and you reach for
your first sheet of top-copy paper. If you have headed paper
printed on A4 giving your name, address and other details,
do not be tempted to use it for the first folio of your copy.

Headed paper is invaluable, if not essential, for letter-
writing where it represents an impression of you as a writer
even before you've written a word on it. What it says and
how the information is laid out gives anyone seeing it an
immediate concept of you, your likely attitude to work
and your probable capability. But for the copy itself it is
wiser to adhere to a more basic first folio: it will look more
businesslike and serve its purpose better.

Let your headed paper state your name clearly in not too
fancy a font without a title (Mr, Mrs, etc.) but with any professional or academic qualifications you may possess. Your
address, telephone number and fax number are the only other
important requirements. I know some writers who also display as part of their credentials a list of magazines they have
contributed to; I don't do this for fear a fixed list would not
be suitable for every letter I might want to write to a variety
of editors in widely different markets.

The facilities both of home computers and in local copy-
shops make the inclusion of little pictures (known to desktop
publishing folk as 'clip-art') simple and appealing. It is easy
to make your name look hand-written or doll up your headed
paper with an excess of logos and monograms and fancy bits.
Please don't over-indulge yourself. Giving a bright and businesslike impression does not depend on gimmicks, although
a modern logo editors associate with a particular writer can
be a help.

While you are getting headed paper printed, don't forget
the same basic design can be used for paper of different sizes:
A5 (half the size of A4, either way up), compliments slips and
business cards. Even small sticky labels can carry a part of
your overall design to keep everything looking like you.

Physical characteristics of copy

Copy sent to an editor should be clean, uncluttered and easy to read. That means using white A4 paper of at least 70 grams in weight. (A4 is 210mm wide by 295mm deep). If you can discover any special likes or dislikes the editor of your intended market has about receiving copy, you'll be in luck. It may surprise you to know, for example, that in this country a number of professionals on newspapers and magazines still work with the 'old' quarto paper.

Don't accept without question the oft quoted recommendation to freelances that the first sheet should indicate only the sender's details with the article's title, wordage and available rights, leaving the article proper to start on the second sheet. In magazine offices such offerings often reveal that the writer is an amateur. Of course there is nothing wrong in being an amateur (who didn't start that way?) but to labour the point is tantamount to saying 'Please give me special consideration because I'm only a beginner.'

It is neater, more sensible and generally acceptable to begin your article, whether you've had previous contact with the editor or not, on folio *one* with what is known as a 'catchline' at the top indicating everything the editor, the copy-taster or anyone else needs to know. Like this:

Jill Dick / Herald / for Jane Brown / Cheese (1200) 1 of 5

This catchline is not underlined but is followed by two blank lines to keep it distinct from the copy itself. It indicates:

- Who the copy is from – in this case, me. (My name or any pseudonym I care to use is known as my 'byline'.)
- The title of the magazine – Herald (in case more than one magazine is dealt with in the same office.)
- The intended recipient – features editor Jane Brown.
- The article is about cheese, is 1200 words long, and this is the first of five folios.

Subsequent sheets carry the same catchline with folio numbers altered as required, although it is not usually necessary to indicate the total length on folios after the first. A 'tag' to identify the article, like 'cheese' in the example above, should befit its substance: copy about cats, for instance, might be identified with 'meow' but be a bit original and don't use

'Christmas' during the festive season when many other pieces besides yours may have the same tag.

So forget that old-hat 'cover-sheet'. Of course it is important to state all relevant information about your copy *somewhere* but what doesn't appear on your catchline is better specified in a short covering letter, if it hasn't already been discussed and settled in earlier correspondence.

All typing must be in double spacing on one side of the sheet only. There should be plenty of white space at the top and foot of each and on both the left and the right of typed text. I generally set my guidelines to leave a minimum 3cm space on the left, 4cm or 4.5 cm at the top and 4cm at the foot.

The space on the right side of the sheet will vary unless the text is 'justified'. That means setting a fixed margin on the right and causing the letters and/or words on each line to be spread out to keep the right edge straight. It is done automatically for body text on the pages of books such as this which would look untidy without it. You will see, too, that every letter is 'proportional' here: the letter 'i', for example, is narrower in print than the letter 'w' and the four-letter word 'till' takes up less space than the four letters in 'maze'. Although modern technology makes proportional typing and justification a simple process, many editors prefer to receive straightforward unjustified text, claiming it is quicker and easier to read. So when your typing machinery produces a right margin that is ragged (meaning not every line ends exactly under the one above) make sure there is a good white space some 3cm or 3.5 cm wide on the right-hand side.

Indent all paragraphs except the first by three or four spaces and write 'more' or 'mf' at the foot of each folio except the last which should end simply with the word 'end'.

A word-processor makes it easy to write at 64 characters (i.e. letters, spaces or punctuation marks) per line and 25 lines per sheet. If you are using a typewriter make a small pencil mark on the paper to remind you when you have typed the 25th line but remember to erase the pencil mark before sending your work out.

You think 64 characters is too short a line and there could be more than 25 lines per sheet? This is a matter of personal preference but, having seen the space most sub-editors need for their instructions to typesetters, layout men, etc., I like to give them plenty.

As for the type itself: whatever your choice of fonts, use the plainest, clearest and neatest your machine can produce and check the ribbon is well inked. Did you hear about the radio station reading out a letter from a listener who said he was 111? There was a pause before the presenter continued. 'No, he's not 111. He's ill.' As ribbons get faint use them for rough drafts and letters to long-suffering friends but always keep a new or re-inked one in your store cupboard.

Punctuation has been touched upon in Chapter 4, but don't be offended if you find your copy has undergone major surgery when it is eventually published. If ever we writers have high horses to get on, it won't be until we are at least in the Graham Greene class. He submitted an essay to a leading Sunday newspaper which returned a proof revealing the insertion of a single comma for the sake of enhanced clarity. The famous writer responded immediately; unless the extra comma was removed he would not allow the piece to be published.

On the paper

If you type an article, other than a very short one, from beginning to end without anything to lighten it (except the indents for new pars) the result can look uninviting, demanding conscious effort of concentration from readers: effort they may not bother to make. Even to an editor's eyes an unbroken slab of text is a burden and that's the last impression you want to convey. Duty tells him to read it and break it up if it's going to be of any use to him. If the writer can't see how dull and boring such unbroken presentation is, he might say to himself, the content of the article is probably just as dull and boring . . .

There are several ways of making your copy look more appetising, even though some may be ignored when the piece is published. Introducing new aspects of the subject matter with subheadings, for example, is effective in softening the text. Subheads are sometimes called 'crossovers' or 'breathers' for obvious reasons. Just as the article's title may be changed so may other aspects of presentation without any reflection on you. Only the sub-editor can know how and where your copy will sit on the page and only he will be in a position to retain, edit or delete your subheads or to insert others elsewhere in your copy if he thinks fit.

Boxes

Boxes come in a different category; you may hear them referred to as 'side-bars' which in essence are the same thing. Imagine you have written an article referring to statistics on, for example, the incidence of car theft in the UK over the past five years. To quote precise figures in the text would slow it up considerably, so it is preferable to put all the factual information together in a ruled box that will appear somewhere on the page beside or beneath the main body of your copy. This way readers can check statistics for themselves with all the information laid before them in one easily assimilated block. There are many articles that benefit from an accompanying 'box' presentation, although more than one or two per article may be over-egging the pudding and give your presentation a 'bitty' appearance. Boxes can hold any useful instruction or data or messages in a brief, crisp and easy-to-read format: lists of ingredients for recipes, for instance, names and addresses of organisations to contact, or a description of how to reach a particular venue named in the body text.

Attracting attention is another reason for using boxes, whatever they contain, and the first person to attract will be the editor. It is best to present a box on a sheet separate from the main article but firmly attached to it with a 'more' indication at the foot of the body text so the box is not overlooked. The word 'end', of course, will then be moved to the foot of the sheet carrying your box.

Bullets and come-ons

In magazine parlance bullets are items of text marked with black blobs or special editorial symbols. Writers use them to draw attention to, for example, a list of objects. Generally it doesn't matter how you highlight such a list and you may prefer to number its items 1, 2, 3, 4, and so on. If your editor obviously likes special symbols (and your typewriter or word-processor can provide them) use them to liven up your presentation and give it variety.

A 'come-on' is just what its name suggests: an editorial device to tell readers it will be worth their while taking notice. A come-on will often be a sentence or a few phrases taken from the copy and repeated in bold type in a ruled or unruled box in the middle of the published article. Although writers do not actively decide what passages in their copy will make good come-ons (that is another job for the sub-editor), wise ones will try to provide plenty of tempting phrases just crying out to be used in this way.

Pins, staples and clips

If you want to annoy the folk dealing with your copy fasten the sheets together with pins to prick their fingers. To be truly beastly get busy with your stapler. That way you offer them the choice of hunting for one of those little gadgets sold specially for unstapling staples, wrecking the ends of paper knives and the like if they don't have the de-staplers to hand, or just pulling stapled sheets apart to leave torn corners – and perhaps torn pages.

Paper-clips are cheap, have no sharp edges, come in plastic or metal, in plain or bright colours and offend nobody. I'm so fond of them I can't bear to part with unusual ones that come my way and one day hope to be the reigning champion (if sole member) of the Unusual Paper-clip Society. Meanwhile I never risk spoiling a good impression (built with hard work and patience) by forgetting what appears trivial but may be important: only use paper-clips to fasten sheets together.

Covering letters

Whether you are going in 'cold' or not and regardless of whether you are submitting a single sheet piece or a twenty-sheet article, enclose a *brief* covering letter. When you submit copy to a magazine it is assumed (without the need to say so directly) that you are offering it for sale, i.e. for financial reward. Do not refer to anything that needs a written reply which will tempt the editor to put the whole package to one side until he or his secretary has time to deal with it, thus losing the immediate impact you are striving for. Observe the following:

- Address it to the correct person (if you don't know the name ring up and ask the switchboard).
- Put your phone number on your letter, as unostentatiously as possible if it doesn't already appear on headed paper bearing your address.
- Get to the point immediately after the Dear X salutation.

- The point will be either: 'Please find enclosed XXX words
  on "Pearl diving in Japan", (or whatever) as agreed in
  our correspondence last month.' This would be a good
  place for a reminder of the agreed fee, if any. If you are
  making an on-spec submission (much as I deplore the
  idea) you could add 'At your usual rates'.
Or
  'Please find enclosed XXX words on "Pearl diving in Japan"
  which I hope you will find of interest.' In the latter case follow with another short par outlining your experience
  and/or knowledge for writing such a piece.
- State what rights you are offering (see Chapter 12).
- State if any pix are enclosed (see Chapter 11).
- Sign off.

Envelopes

Your copy is perfectly presented and you're ready to put it in
the envelope – at last. If it is short enough to be carried on a
single sheet, folding it into three for a 22cm x 11cm envelope
will suffice. For two or three sheets I recommend folding once
to A5 size in an envelope of the same size and for copy of
more than three sheets you should use an envelope large
enough to take the entire pack without folding. You must also
be sure your envelope is adequately stamped. At a car-boot
sale I bought an envelope-weighing machine which has
proved its worth many times the 50 pence it cost. When your
package includes pix make sure they are sandwiched between
stiff card or padding for protection.

If you have had no previous contact with the magazine
you should enclose a stamped self-addressed envelope. Why
should anyone reply if you don't? Stamps and envelopes
cost money. Even if you have been in earlier contact with the
editor or someone on his staff I advise sending a SAE: it
is a mistake to presume on what might be a relationship
less firm than you think it is, the person you dealt with before
may have gone away and, in any case, politeness always
pays.

Despatch

Whatever rules and tips you read or hear, remember this one:
it is truly the most important of all:

NEVER PART WITH THE ONLY COPY OF YOUR WORK

Terrible tales are told by unfortunate writers who have left the only copy of an article/short story/novel/radio play, etc. on a bus or a train, in a café or a shop. Some thieves and burglars even stoop as low as to ignore the family silver and make off with uncopied manuscripts, depriving the writer of what he treasures most and insurance companies can never replace. Unless you want to experience such a nightmare *always* make a copy of everything you write. It doesn't matter whether you use old carbon paper to provide a smudgy blue or black copy as your write or type, whether you frequent a traditional copy-shop or whether you have the most sophisticated disk-copying method money can buy: only the security of having a copy (or more than one copy if this paragraph makes you nervous) safely tucked away in a separate place will allow you to sleep easily in your bed.

Don't wait until you lose your only copy. There is a law that decrees you will lose it if it's the only one you have. I can't explain why, if you have at least one other copy, the law doesn't apply.

11
Pix

Countless articles in magazines would never see the light of day were they not accompanied by good photographs; and 'good' in this sense means they are just what the editor wants and better than he could find for himself. The latter point is particularly worth noting, for why should he pay you unless your pix (as they are commonly called) are better than those his own sources can provide? All consumer magazines have access to their own stocks of assorted pictures or can buy what they want from agencies and libraries established for the purpose of supplying the press. Some have their own staff photographers who will inevitably be better acquainted with what the editor wants than you can ever be.

So it is wise to leave the obtaining of pix to the editor if you suspect the best you can provide will be less than acceptable in quality or relevance to your topic. Illustrations are not confined to photographs; accomplished cartoonists or writers who can supply their own artwork are ideally placed to offer editors something eye-catching, unique – and readily acceptable.

There is no doubt the majority of magazines would barely survive without illustrations. Dull slabs of prose can be decidedly unattractive, no matter how inventive the sub-editors might be in trying to break them up and lighten their impact. Because illustrations are desperately needed and appropriately targeted articles with accompanying pix often find good homes, offering editors a double package increases your chances of making regular sales at good rates and your ratio of sales to submissions will improve.

Which comes first?

Which is more important, the picture or the story? Because the opportunities in selling illustrated articles (photo-journalism) are limitless there are many articles that begin as an image in the writer's mind rather than as a story-that-must-be-told. It matters not which comes first but there is a subtle distinction between a picture telling a story and an article with supporting pix. When the picture *is* the article the emphasis will be on what is illustrated; text will be underwriting, expanding, perhaps supplying historical background or whatever is appropriate. So while most writers assume pix are merely useful additional features, those who occasionally reverse the commonplace and present editors with good pictures promoted by illustrative text can find a ready welcome.

Whichever your choice and however your article is prepared, the reader must know at a glance exactly what it is about. That means not only must the opening words grab the attention but the accompanying pix must also be an immediate hook.

Types of Pictures

To have a fair chance of selling, a picture must have an instant appeal. That means even a glance will stop casual readers and focus their attention on the page. Remember that is the main purpose of pix accompanying articles and you won't forget the importance of only submitting those of the right type:

- Of high quality with sharp detail.
- Conforming to your chosen magazine's format and size.
- Frequently of happy, healthy people engaged in some task relevant to the theme of your article.
- Perhaps close-ups of your subject matter.
- With an unusual slant if the market favours such pix.
- Explaining or enlightening the text.
- A pic that simply can't be passed by.

Using other people's pix

Submit photographs you've taken from an old magazine as if they were yours and you invite trouble. It makes no difference if the magazine was published years ago or even if you've seen the same pix several times in a variety of magazines. Don't copy from advertisements either. Back in 1887 the manufacturers of Pears soap infuriated art lovers by using a copy of the famous picture 'Bubbles' by Sir John Millais and adapting an old *Punch* illustration to publicise their latest brand of soap. Try such 'borrowing' and you will do more than annoy someone: the law, quite rightly, has redress for those whose copyright is infringed.

Every published photograph belongs either to the person who took it, i.e. the photographer, or (if the magazine who bought it for use on the first occasion paid the photographer to surrender all rights in it) to the magazine publishing it. Regardless of who holds the right to reproduce the picture, if you try to sell what is not yours without permission you will be guilty of theft and attempting to defraud the rightful owner. In some photographic circles the buyer of the film is credited with ownership of copyright, even if the subsequent pictures were taken by a different person. This point has been known to cause difficulties for photographers able to claim expenses from magazines and newspapers, so don't be too eager to unload the cost of film on an editor who might be willing to subsidise you. Elsewhere, in certain circumstances, the person being photographed, if the target is a person, is deemed to have a share in the copyright, although (thankfully) this odd ruling has never been upheld.

So you see just the picture you want on a picture postcard or in an old book you thumb through at a car-boot sale. How can you use it without incurring somebody's wrath?

For the latter, if you can be certain the book is over fifty years old and out of copyright, you may use its pix with impunity. But be careful. The copy in your hand may have been published more than fifty years ago according to the date on the flyleaf, but there may have been new editions you know nothing about that are not out of copyright and carry the same pix. A cautious writer will contact the publishers, if they are still in business, and ask for written permission to use the picture. If that is impossible and you can't find the rightful owner of the copyright you might decide to take a chance. I don't advise it, but if you do you should at least include a credit to the original publisher when you submit the pix to a magazine. For picture postcards the same rule applies except that, again, you may not be able to find the original publisher and holder of the copyright.

Notwithstanding copyright problems, selling old pictures (as well as new) for reproduction is a thriving business for the many picture libraries up and down the country, as outlined below. You will have to pay a fee for each picture you want to use (and writers often complain the fees are higher than they should be) but at least using pix acquired through the proper channels won't cause you any headaches: it is better to be safe, even if a little poorer, than sorry.

Where and how to get them

When you submit pix to a magazine it is assumed you have the right to do so (but see below) and that the pictures are yours. This being so, they should have your credentials on the back clearly identifying them as your property. But what if they are not good enough?
Here are four ways of setting to work:

- Improve your camera technique.
- Obtain free pix from other sources.
- Rent or buy from agencies and picture libraries.
- Put photographers and editors in touch with each other and let them make their own arrangements.

Improve your camera technique

Modern technology boosts sagging confidence; many 35mm compact automatic cameras ask you only to point at the target in the viewfinder, press a button – and there's success. Such pictures form the majority of those accepted by magazines. Adding a zoom lens makes the target appear closer without the photographer having to move any nearer and is equally painless to use. An automatic single-lens reflex camera (known as an SLR) on which you can interchange lenses is ideal. For simple operation choose one offering manual focusing. There are dozens of cameras more sophisticated and complicated but if you are a writer first and a photographer very much second, the above set-up will suffice and produce perfectly good results.

This is not a book on photography so if you are happy devoting your time to photography rather than writing, you should seek out the many specialist magazines and books for amateur photographers, regular and careful study of which will teach you a great deal.

Beginners should stick to black and white film. To satisfy editors, almost everyone could stick to black and white. With the exception of publications specialising in colour or using it for particular displays, magazines generally prefer to deal with plain black and white. For general work colour prints are seldom wanted; the results are often substandard and magazines that do use colour pix are likely to prefer transparencies.

Whatever your camera choice, automatic or manual, always carry enough film and then some more because it is wise to take several shots of everything you photograph if you can. Although of the same topic they will differ from each other and each will therefore be original.

In photographic terms 'framing' refers to how adequately the picture fills the space available for it; we are not talking here about any contraption for hanging the picture on the wall or standing it on the mantelpiece.

Filling the frame means letting your target, the subject of the picture, do just that. Always see there is as little wasted space as possible around the target. This ensures the eye is not distracted by fuzzy images at the edge of the photograph and sharpens the target itself. Here, the picture says with impact, is what it's all about – and nothing else.

What if the target is too large for the frame and a shot of it all will be unacceptably small? Simply take part of it only and let that fill the frame.

Developing

Processing your own film is a time-consuming business and can be quite costly, particularly when you start. Writer-photographers usually find it better to forget ideas of doing it themselves and devote their time to writing and taking the shots; when it comes to developing film the cobbler should stick to his last.

Take your used film along to the local chemist or high-street developer and you'll have to wait for it to be returned, risk having it lost or even (as has happened to me twice) receive someone else's film back in place of yours. Worse, even what look like 'good' pix acquired this way are unlikely to reproduce to the high standards required for use by many consumer magazines. Gone are the hit-and-miss days when photos might not 'come out' properly but your own work in taking the pix can easily be lost by poor developing. Remember, in deciding whether to accept or reject pictures, pay you for them or buy them from elsewhere, the editor's first yardstick is quality.

Far better is to approach an established photography shop where you will often find advice and help as well as a professional contact print service. Ask for just a sheet of contact prints first. These are small pictures printed directly from the negatives and will give you a chance to decide which of your prints is/are best for the market you are submitting to and the article you have written or plan to write. A black and white print should be no less that 8½″ by 6½″ (wholeplate size) and preferably larger with the surface unscratched.

Obtain free pix from other sources

Pictures tell stories. So large companies wishing to promote their wares are usually happy to supply writers with pictures absolutely free. There may be a hope that you include reference to the company at the foot of the picture when it is published and you should explain that you will do so, although you cannot be responsible if such a reference does not appear when the picture is eventually published.

Rent or buy from agencies and picture libraries

Research for pictures is as specialised a task as is research in any other field. Picture researchers have their own organisation (the Society of Picture Researchers and Editors) and most of the sources they consult are professionally organised, and belong to the British Association of Picture Libraries (BAPLA, see below). Libraries and agencies hold huge stocks of photographs to loan to customers who might include magazines, book publishers and individual writers. Some establishments offer an additional service that can be invaluable; for an agreed extra fee they will send their own photographers (or freelances whose work they know) to take particular photographs for a special assignment.

So vast is the range of photographs held by large picture libraries that smaller ones compete by holding stocks of pictures covering a certain topic – marine life, say, or mountaineering – and they often become well known suppliers of such pix. Hiring unusual or specialised pictures can be expensive so it is best to establish with an editor before doing so whether he wants to buy the article, whether he expects you to supply the pictures to go with it – and who is to pay for them.

Broadly speaking, picture libraries fall into three main categories:

Press Agencies and general picture libraries. These are wholly commercial enterprises with huge stocks to be hired by anyone and everyone. They are usually run efficiently and speedily, being much patronised by national newspapers who cannot afford to wait, and can obtain pictures from almost anywhere in the world. Needless to say, such services are costly.

Connoisseur or specialised collections. These collections cover topics large and small, exotic and quaint, humdrum and precious, from far and near. The staff they employ are experts who can usually find exactly what you want. They can also tell you what you will *never* find, no matter where or how hard you look. (There is, for instance, no genuine picture of playwright Christopher Marlowe.)

National archives and museums. Although Britain has a high proportion of the world's finest pictures the keepers of public institutions are not renowned for their readiness in helping press photographers. They will hire out the pictures in their charge but writers often find obtaining them is laborious, frustrating and, possibly because conservation does not sit comfortably with commercial leasing, barely worth the struggle.

Making use of picture libraries is not the sole prerogative of magazines and newspapers. Anyone can hire pix for a fee providing due acknowledgement is made for their use.

If your first contact is by telephone make sure you know exactly what you are looking for. Your request could be either specific (a picture of Charles Dickens, for example) or general but on a particular topic. You might need a selection of pix to support an article about, say, Victorian and Edwardian corsetry and will only know what you want when you see it. Call at the library yourself if you can as nobody else can make the ideal choice for you. But if personal visiting is impossible the library staff will do their best and send you the most promising selection they can find. For such work (which may take hours and involve complex research) you will be charged a search fee before being presented with an assortment from which to choose. When you make your choice most libraries allow lower rates for multiple selection.

It is important to understand whether you are hiring pictures, i.e. they have to be returned, or buying them outright when of course there is nothing to return. Ask for a copy of rates and borrowing conditions before you start so you know exactly what your commitment will be. Is there a holding fee per day, per week or how does the library estimate its charges? And take care of any prints or transparencies you have only borrowed because you will be charged a high price if they are damaged when you return them. Whichever way your chosen library works, you may also be asked where the pix will be published (or you hope they will be published if you have not yet reached an agreement with an editor). Many agencies and libraries charge standard fees according to magazine advertising rates; you could hardly expect to hire a pic for *Homes and Gardens* for the same price as one for your local church magazine. Alas, sob stories about not being able to sell the pix after all fall on deaf ears.

Always keep in mind just what the pictures you want are for. Except on rare occasions they are a support and extension of your written work, but nothing more. So be careful not to get so carried away with what you find in a picture library that the cost of the pix exceeds their value *to your project*. It is not sensible to let the tail wag the dog.

CD libraries

In today's high-technology world picture libraries use another valuable and increasingly popular method of storing pix. CD-ROM is a computerised system which packs a vast array of pictures on a compact disk which can be read by any appropriate machine such as those made by Commodore, Amstrad, Apple, Atari, Macintosh or PC compatibles.

The word 'ROM' means 'read only memory' which restricts the user to looking at, not copying, saving or editing, the contents of ROM, be that pictures, text, fonts, information or whatever the manufacturer chooses to put on the compact disk. But the more advanced CD libraries have developed a technique to release sections of compact disks so that (when an extra fee is paid) the user can copy, i.e. save, a selected picture for his own use. The system still has its problems: CD-ROM pictures designed for eventual printing need sharper resolution and occupy more space on the disk than those intended only for screen display. So there will be more pix on a 'black and white' disk than on a 'colour' one and the cost of 'renting' a particular picture, if your chosen library offers this service, will be lower for B/W than for colour.

Happily, to remain competitive, picture libraries need their stocks constantly replenished and updated. That means any photographer can sell high-quality pix to them as well as hire from them. If your own photographs are in this class, contacting libraries and agencies (offering transparencies rather than prints) may prove a valuable source of extra income. But be warned: the quality required for success in selling to libraries is very high. Only the best will do.

Put photographers and editors in touch with each other and let them make their own arrangements

For writers who do not take their own pix there is another solution. When an editor asks for accompanying pictures or assumes they will be provided ('You will send me some pictures, won't you?'), simply locate a photographer and put him in touch with the editor. Keep both fully in the picture (oops, sorry) and let the editor strike whatever deal he likes and pay the photographer directly for any pictures bought. That way you can concentrate on the writing of the piece and leave the pictures to other people who know more about it than you do.

Captions

Always name and number your pix. This is particularly important as your collection grows and even when you start will enable easy identification of individual prints by everybody handling them.

Keep such identification as simple as possible. The parent article can be a number, for example, with its attendant pix lettered accordingly. If your article record book (see Chapter 12) lists articles by number, keeping track of what you have sent where and what has happened to it, tying your pix to articles this way is logical and keeps everything clear and tidy. Thus 14A and 14B could be pictures A and B from a sheet of contact prints taken to accompany article 14 about, for example, gravestones; 38C could be the best illustration for copy (article

38 in your records) telling the story of a young violinist prodigy. Attach small labels bearing the identification codes on the back of each pic, being careful to write the labels first so as not to damage the prints.

To connect your pictures to their captions merely list on a separate piece of paper the identification codes with the captions you want to appear:

14A Lord Templetwist – high and mighty even in death.
14B Mother died first, leaving spaces for her seven children.
38C The world's smallest violin made for two-year-old fingers.

Keeping records

If your collection of photographs grows very large it might demand a separate record book. There might also be pix that do not have written copy to cling to and stand as sales in their own right. It is time to open a 'picture book'. However you choose to organise it, adopt an identification system different from that used for copy so you won't confuse the two in writing to editors, claiming payment, offering rights, etc. Simple record-keeping is always preferable to a complex highly technical method you can't understand at a glance when you come back from holiday and your mind's a blank.

The physical storage of photographs and negatives is more complex than keeping written copy. But a stout file with plastic pockets will hold individual pix or contact sheets quite adequately, while smaller strips of negatives can be stored in little see-through sleeves for instant and easy identification.

Rights

Imagine photographer A takes a picture, develops it (or has someone else develop it) and sells a magazine the right to use it once in its pages. This option on a *single use* can be sold again and again, much as a hire car may be hired out to different people any number of times. This procedure is, of course, quite different from the selling of text where first rights are exhausted after the initial sale, leaving only second, third rights – in theory if not practice – as dwindling negotiable assets.

Alternatively a magazine buying a picture being sold for the first time from photographer B may offer him a higher fee for handing over all rights in the pic. If he accepts he relinquishes any further claim and can earn no more fees from it, however many times and wherever it may be reproduced in the future.

Who is better off, photographer A or photographer B? That depends on the innate value of the picture, how many times it is likely to sell and for how much.

When you sell an editor one of your pix be sure to make it clear you are offering him a chance to reproduce it once and once only for an agreed fee. Never part with copyright, i.e. hand over full unfettered use to anyone. Pictures you have taken are *yours* and should remain so. You never know when the subject may suddenly become fashionable, not to say famous, and then . . . Imagine the chagrin if you had sold all rights in your pictures at such a time!

All for nothing?

Despite advice to the contrary (from me as well as from other people) a high proportion of articles are still submitted to magazines *on spec*. So are pictures which tend to cause more trouble than copy. They get lost, their ownership is disputed, they are published without credit and too often they are either not paid for or are lumped into an overall fee. A picture may or may not be worth a thousand words but on the whole it is more difficult and expensive to replace.

In common with all writing practice negotiation with magazine editors best comes before doing the job. If there has been no editorial contact and your illustrated article is published, you might expect to receive one fee for the copy and an extra one for the pix. If this is not what you receive you may only have yourself to blame; at this stage it is too late to alter the situation and you'll just have to take whatever you are given.

Since enclosing or not enclosing pix with an article may make the difference between acceptance or rejection, an editor may consider the pix form an integral part of the whole submission and therefore do not merit a separate fee. Such thoughts easily persuade him to pay, in effect, nothing for the pictures you may have taken and tended so carefully or even paid someone else to supply.

On the other hand, if you enjoy photography and feel your skills will improve with practice, there might be at least two valid reasons for continuing to submit them even if they attract no extra fee: you will never actually know whether the article would have been accepted without them, and publication of your pix is valuable when you want proof of your success to show editors in higher-paying markets in the future.

Some useful contacts and sources

BAPLA, British Association of Picture Libraries and Agencies, 13 Woodberry Crescent, London N10 1PJ. Tel: 081-444 7913. Publishes a comprehensive annual directory of its members, an invaluable aid for all picture users. Also a quarterly news journal and other publications.

The Picture Researcher's Handbook, compiled by Hilary and Mary Evans, Chapman & Hall Ltd, 2–6 Boundary Row, London SE1 8HN. Tel: 071-865 0066. The standard reference book for picture sources listing more than 1000.

Barnaby's Picture Library, 19 Rathbone Street, London W1P 1AF. Tel: 071-636 6128. Houses more than 4,000,000 pictures on a huge variety of topics.

The Press Association Photos, 85 Fleet Street, London EC4P 4BE. Tel: 071-353 7440. The news picture service of the Press Association.

The Association of Photographers, 9–10 Domingo Street, London EC1Y 0TA. Tel: 071-608 1441. For the serious photographer only.

The Bureau of Freelance Photographers, Focus House, 497 Green Lanes, London N13 4BP. Tel: 081-882 3315. Publishes a monthly *Market Newsletter* for members, giving details of current markets, etc. and offers a free advisory service. Also publishes *The Freelance Photographer's Market Handbook*.

12
The business of selling

If you have never worked in a magazine office or known any-one who has done so, a brief explanation of how solicited and unsolicited manuscripts are received may be helpful. I have heard editors despair at the poor salesmanship of many writers hoping to sell their work and I've also listened to rejected writers who suspect their work has been returned unread. Both editors and writers have cause to sigh at such misunderstand-ing. We have discussed how to present each piece of work so its arrival raises rather than dampens editorial spirits. But there is more to it than that . . .

The right ingredients

Throughout this book we've discussed the best recipe for success in writing. Now we talk about the best recipe for suc-cess in *selling*: the adoption of a confident and professional attitude.

How editors think

Try to imagine yourself as an editor. You have all the pages of a magazine to fill every week or month, or whenever frequency of publication decrees, and how well it is done rests entirely on your shoulders. There will be other people work-ing with you, except on the very smallest periodicals, but the ultimate responsibility for triumph or failure is yours. Filling those pages to meet editorial and advertising policy is far from easy. What happens if you are dependent on freelance copy and don't receive enough you can accept? What hap-pens, frankly, is that you are soon called in to explain to your superiors why readers are no longer eager and circulation is falling.

So the editor is desperate to receive good copy and you are keen to write it. Isn't it absurd that we can't marry the two factors together every time? Too often the reason is even more absurd: that writers and editors do not understand each other and have not learned how to improve their relationships.

I sometimes think diplomacy should be among required training for freelances. It is defined in *The Chambers Dictionary* as 'tact in management of people concerned in any affair'. Yet many writers post off query letters or unsolicited copy, which is worse, without making the most rudimentary attempts at 'tact in management of people concerned'. The importance of making your copy give the right impression has been covered in Chapter 10 but here are a few points aimed at pleasing the inner man as well as the outer market:

- Ring the switchboard to ask when is the most convenient time to phone the editor or the person you are dealing with – and confirm his name.
- Ask the editor's secretary to send you a sheet of copy dates, offering a stamped addressed envelope, of course. These indicate the flow of copy and everything else, showing what is in the pipeline and where at any given date or time. The more clearly you understand the timing of copy-flow, the less trouble you are likely to cause.
- If working after favourable response to a query, don't ring with further questions or problems unless absolutely necessary.
- Never forget that the editor is always right.

Query letters

Listen to writers talking and you will hear opinions divided about whether to query an editor concerning an article before you write it or to submit it in 'ready to use' form without prior contact.

Although I've advised against submitting 'on spec', the truth is that both approaches work at different times and for different magazines. Only trial and error, aided by a bit of experienced judgement, can persuade you to try one way or the other. There may be occasions when the pace eases in a normally busy editorial office and the editor is happy to read, consider and reply to letters discussing what he might like to see for future issues. At other times he could be so busy that all he wants is a complete, acceptable, and 'ready to go' piece of work sitting on his desk. It would be misleading to lay down any hard-and-fast rule.

One writer friend always begins with query letters, vowing they generally lead to sales. As few UK magazines issue prospective contributors with a list of topics already in the pipeline for future issues, a custom favoured by an increasing number of US markets, the query letter may be a valuable aid for writers who do not want to waste time and effort preparing material that will inevitably be rejected.

Other freelances think query letters are too easily put aside in favour of acceptable copy in the editor's hand. While there is nothing to beat offering the right piece to the right editor at the right time, which is what we all aim for, such tactics can fail. If the copy – from large numbers of freelances – is not right, the editor is swamped with unsuitable, unwelcome and unacceptable material. An avalanche of unusable copy landing on editorial desks is counter-productive to all of us. It brands senders as perpetual amateurs with more time than sense and blocks channels of communication. Ultimately this only makes it harder for copy *with the professional touch* to be located and considered.

A query letter as the first shot in your sales armoury gives its recipient an immediate impression. It tells him you can express yourself in uncluttered logic, you have a proper understanding of his magazine and its requirements and you can be relied on to supply what you offer. So before sending it you should work on it quite as carefully as you will on the copy you subsequently write. Keep the letter brief and to the point. Address the editor by name as 'Mr Taylor' or 'John Taylor' but not, at least until on familiar terms and then only with discretion, as 'John'. Doubts about the marital status of a female editor are best resolved by ringing the magazine switchboard and asking how the lady prefers to be addressed.

Outline your article idea clearly and succinctly but in sufficient detail for its potential to be assessed. Include a short synopsis of how you intend to cover the subject (a précis of the contents of each section and/or paragraph should suffice) and state the intended length. Give the date by which you could submit your copy and add details of your past successes especially in relevant fields. Remember, of course, to include an SAE for the editor's reply.

Selling your idea on the phone is not easy and not to be

recommended if you are completely unknown. Even when you have had prior contact with the editor or someone on his staff you have no way of judging how much attention your phoned sales-pitch will receive, for you cannot know just what is happening in the office at the time you choose to ring. So I advise against trying to sell an idea this way. Too often it results in either a suggestion that you 'Put it in an envelope to us, will you?' or a (probably) well-meant promise of 'We'll think about it and let you know'. In the former case the call has gained you nothing and may have interrupted and irked the person you were speaking to and in the latter nothing further may happen.

Commissioned work

I recently heard a writer saying he was unsure about whether he had actually been given a commission or not. An editor was interested in his proposal and suggested he should go away, do the job and come back with the completed copy. Was this a 'commission'? If that is a precise account of the editor's response the answer is undoubtedly 'No'. A commission or contract is a firm promise of *intent to publish*, nothing more nothing less, and it matters not whether it is delivered by letter, over the telephone or face to face.

Commissions are not easily won even by experienced freelances. For an editor to commit his magazine to publishing something he has not yet seen he must be convinced the writer can and will provide exactly what is wanted at the right time. Suppose the most highly skilled writer whose work is well known and has been published many times turns in copy below the expected standard, has an accident or is suddenly unable to fulfil expectations? Ask yourself this: if you were an editor, would you feel confident in granting commissions?

The truth is that in today's magazine scene freelance commissions are less frequently offered than they used to be. But that does not mean you may not be asked to fill a particular spot or make a regular contribution. When that happens it is important to understand the invitation: it is unlikely to encompass a promise to print whatever you write (i.e. is not a contract) for the editor will retain the option on rejecting your copy if he considers it unsuitable. But for most such contributors the invitation does embrace the promise to pay a fee.

If you are in any doubt about your position you should always ask for a simple explanation.

A couple of brief warnings: don't make heavy weather of your rights and demands – a light but *privately serious* approach best sorts out initial misunderstandings. And remember that even an agreed regular spot may quickly be withdrawn if you let the magazine down.

Rights to sell – and to keep

Everything you write is born with its own set of rights, the most basic of which is 'copyright'. It reserves for you the ownership of the piece, in law, and prevents other people from reproducing it exactly as you have written it, claiming it as theirs and receiving payment for it. Note those words *exactly as you have written it* on which most arguments about infringement of copyright founder. If someone uses your *idea* or writes about it in similar vein he is guilty of no infringement. There is no copyright in ideas and no restriction on writing about something already in print. If there were, the world of literature and letters would be minuscule indeed.

When you work as a freelance and sell copy to a magazine you retain the copyright in the piece (see below) but offer the magazine the first right to publish in this country, an offer known as First British Rights. You can call these 'Serial Rights' if you wish, although the word 'serial' is something of an anachronism nowadays. It originally related to the publication of a story running in several parts or successive editions of a magazine, i.e. in 'series' and is less common in modern usage.

There are cases where a magazine may try to buy All Rights from you, and that includes your copyright, but such endeavours should be resisted. Hand over your copyright and you forfeit the chance to claim against anyone using your work in its original form as well as the chance to recoup any fees paid for its subsequent publication. Fortunately attempts at outright buying of copyright are not frequent but if you are faced with such a demand a simple action removes it: cross out any claim on the back of a cheque (or in any other correspondence) about a company buying 'All Rights' and bank the cheque as usual. In doing so you are risking nothing, for an attempt by a magazine to take All Rights without your permission is illegal. If you're still uneasy take comfort from the fact that the great majority of writers happily published in magazines never meet this problem at all.

As there are First British Rights to offer to magazines when you submit copy for its first use in any British publication (and that includes newspapers), so there are, in theory, second, third – and so on – rights to offer with each subsequent sale of the identical piece. In practice nobody will buy copy already published elsewhere, or if they do the rewards will hardly pay for the postage, so you may forget about any rights other than the first.

Discussing money

Never be afraid to talk about what you will be paid for accepted copy. 'I might upset them and then they won't want me' or 'I'll take anything at first until I get on firmer ground' are understandable fears beginners voice: understandable but short-sighted. Magazine publication is a business and operates as such. Its employees, and that includes freelances, are as much engaged in a 'proper' job as are postmen, solicitors, garage mechanics or anybody else. Do you not mention the salary when you apply for a job? Are you happy to accept low pay until your employer decides you might have more? Such a weak approach in discussing money is guaranteed to keep you at the bottom of the ladder.

What a magazine pays its contributors depends on several factors, among them:

- Company policy (generally determined by the financial state of the proprietors or parent group).
- Negotiated agreements with the National Union of Journalists (NUJ) and/or any other bodies.
- The writer's likely future value to the magazine.
- How little individual freelances will accept.

I'm sorry to have to include the last point but, sadly, I have found it to be valid. It is a fact that some markets (not all, by any means) offer a beginning freelance a derisory fee or invite him to state what he wants to be paid. Either way the poor writer is in a spot: if he doesn't know the standard rates he can neither assess the offer nor suggest a figure of his own. The solution lies in investigating the fees position *before* getting into such a predicament.

The majority of magazines have negotiated settlements with the NUJ who issue a comprehensive guide detailing what freelances should be paid. Copies are obtainable (enclose an SAE 10″ by 7″) from:

NUJ, Freelance Sector, Acorn House, 314 Gray's Inn Road, London WC1X 8DP.

When discussing fees with an editor you should also ask when you will be paid. Most magazines have standard procedures varying according to their publication frequency and sometimes dependent on their circulation. Payment at the end of the month following publication is common but does not always materialise. If you feel uneasy at pressing the matter with an editor ask to see or speak to someone in the accounts department. If no definite publication date has been agreed for your copy you should ask that payment be made by a specified date – in four weeks' time, perhaps, or at the end of the month of publication.

Straightening out the matter with the people whose job it is to issue cheques also gives you an opportunity to ensure yours is made out correctly. In early 1993 most of the main clearing banks announced new measures to protect themselves and their customers against fraud. One change is particularly important for writers who use pen names. Banks now issue chequebooks crossed 'A/C Payee only'. So if you write under a pseudonym check that the accounts department makes out the cheque in the same name as the person holding the bank account.

The waiting

The busy atmosphere generally prevailing in editorial offices partly explains why writers who submit unsolicited copy have to be patient. You despatched an article to a magazine and the result is – nothing.

Why does it take editors so long to choose, as their first decision, whether they want it or not? Several no-nonsense editors claim it takes but a moment to spot a real no-hoper and slip it back in the SAE for quick rejection. Others toiling under hefty daily deliveries of mail confess their office staff can't cope and it is common for submissions to stay in heaps on the floor for weeks. Some magazines find this frustrating and receive so much harassment from writers they genuinely try to relieve the situation. A few have announced they will only accept unsolicited work on stated dates and several others refuse anything that has not been under discussion. In such cases an editor or one of his staff may have expressed willingness to read the copy (nothing more, and certainly with no commitment having been made) and will provide a writer with a code number to put on the envelope carrying the relevant copy. When it arrives it can easily be sorted from other non-coded submissions and should at least be dealt with fairly promptly.

In spite of these occasional helpful attempts at easing the problem it is not uncommon for six months to pass before a writer is given any idea of what has happened to his work. A handful I know decided enough was enough and it was time to take a more practical line; they now put a time limit on all unsolicited work, enclosing a polite but firm note indicating it will remain on offer to the editor until a stated date. How far ahead of submission that date is will depend on the publication frequency of the magazine but for a monthly it is usually about nine or ten weeks ahead.

You may think that is cutting off the nose to spite the face but any novel ideas you may have about how to get editors to respond could be worth a try.

More waiting . . .

At last comes the decision and your copy has been accepted. But when the news is good there may be more delay, this time for publication which may take months; I've had complaints from some writing friends who have had to wait for *years*. Advice on how to speed up this stage? Realistically there are only two courses of action and one of those is unthinkable. You can either demand your copy back and forget the whole business (well, who would do that after going to such trouble?) or you can sit tight, make polite enquiry about progress ('in case I missed seeing it') and busy yourself with other work.

And yet more . . .

The patience of writers is still put to the test after publication and perhaps this is the hardest and least reasonable delay to endure: waiting for payment. To obtain what is our due we sometimes have to resort to strong words, to threats of starting action in the courts and even to taking those first steps in suing magazine owners or proprietors. If you reach the point of having to threaten court action (and you must be prepared to go ahead with such a plan if it becomes necessary), write by Recorded Delivery to the accounts department, addressed to the Chief Accountant if the magazine is part of a large group, telling him what you intend to do. Mark your letter 'Recorded Delivery' so the seriousness of the position is still evident if the envelope is thrown away. State that you will proceed to the County Court unless you receive payment for X script (the title of your unpaid work) by a stated date three or four weeks ahead of the date of your letter.

It is a comfort to report that most of the writers questioned in my research on this topic found the threat of court action enough to make cheques appear in their letter-boxes as if by magic.

All the same who wants to have to threaten legal action every time a magazine is slow to pay? There can hardly be any other commodity that is sold on such a curious basis; that an unstated fee will be paid for it at some unspecified time if the editor then decides he wants it; or it may be torn up, abandoned or discarded without recompense to the writer. How, you may ask, are we writers ever going to get out of this unsatisfactory state?

I believe there are ways of improving our chances in the editorial pot. Among them are careful marketing, quality writing, painstaking research and all the other points raised in these pages. Given these elements, the single most effective additional aid is to do business in as professional a manner as possible.

Have you ever wondered why so many editors treat writers badly? I have had years of seeing both sides of this writing game; working in editorial offices *and* getting to know how some non-professional writers think. And I use the term 'non-professional' here in its depressing sense, meaning writers who persist in behaving like amateurs even though they are not necessarily beginners. Such folk happily accept low or even *no* fees for their work, having learned that some editors will take their free or virtually free copy even if someone on the staff has to smarten it up before it is ready for publication.

As long as these 'perpetual amateurs' exist there is no

incentive for editors to treat writers any better than they do now – so they won't. Ah, you might argue, but why not be a 'perpetual amateur' if you can get published that way without much difficulty? Well, it depends on what you want as a writer. I could accept derisory fees or give my copy away. But I can't separate being a writer from working at a professional job which satisfies both my bank balance and my self-respect. If you aren't fussy about either . . .

So let's consider some practical answers to this apparently endless waiting game editors often make us play. Always address your cash queries to the accounts department of the magazine, rather than the editorial, thereby tackling the appropriate people while not prejudicing any future relationships with the editor. Present your invoice neatly and without frills, on your headed paper, perhaps like this:

INVOICE (give number)   (today's date)

Copy: Carsington Water 1200 wds + 3 pix
Published: Reservoir Magazine July 1994
Fee due: £185.00
Payment date: 29 July 1994

Give the invoice a number and a date, sign it and be sure to keep a copy in your records.

If nothing happens after a month (in the case of a monthly publication: in a fortnight if publication is more frequent) send another invoice marked SECOND INVOICE in red and enclose a copy of the first. But supposing even your best and most professional endeavours to obtain what is rightly yours comes to naught? Is it time to be *un*professional?

On various occasions I and colleagues have tried patience, polite persistence, not-so-polite persistence, downright brusque persistence, threatening to sue and actually suing. Mostly the stronger the action the better the results; it is a sad fact, and not only in the world of writing, that those who shout loudest usually receive the best attention. But several times unorthodox and 'Oh, you can't do that!' tactics have proved more effective than any of the above.

Here are a few you might care to try when owed money and sufficiently driven by frustration, starvation or general outrage:

• If a fee has been negotiated send an invoice to the

accounts department for double the agreed amount or at least more than you expect.

- Urge a recognised body such as the National Union of Journalists or the Society of Authors to publish a list of bad payers – and see the baddie who owes you money is on it.
- Inform the magazine that you are writing a report (and do so) for a writers' journal, or similar, listing poor payers in the magazine field. You do hope you won't have to include . . .
- 1 Attend the editorial or accounts office in person.
  2 Do not announce you are coming.
  3 Take with you a fretful baby, an inexhaustible toddler or an impatient dog (or any combination of the three) and make no effort to quieten or control any of them.
  4 Ask staff members to hold the baby, amuse the toddler or calm the dog while you sort out your papers.
  5 If you can't find live companions take sandwiches, a vacuum flask and a radio.
  6 Stay until your account is paid, however, long it takes. No magazine can risk the bad publicity of having you evicted by force nor can you be left in the office alone at night with free access to equipment and telephones.

Kill fees

It rarely happens that an editor accepts your copy and then changes his mind. But it might be that he finds something on similar lines that he likes better, the circumstances in which your copy was appropriate no longer obtain or, as is his prerogative, he just doesn't want it any more. If this happens after your work has clearly been accepted either verbally or by letter you should be paid what is known as a 'kill' fee. How much this is may be determined by standard editorial practice for the magazine concerned, or its parent group, or may be left to the editor's discretion. Since it represents a loss to the magazine you may not receive much but justice demands you get something. If a kill fee is not forthcoming, and few editors will offer one unless you raise the matter first, point out the difficulties you may have in selling the piece elsewhere, especially if it was researched and angled at the request of the magazine now killing it. Be polite and firm if you want fair treatment.

When commissioned or accepted copy is unused and a kill fee has been paid for its non-use the original rights in it remain untouched. It has never been published so you are free to offer first rights again wherever you choose without any requirement, legal or ethical, to mention its history.

Keeping records the easy way

It is easy to keep records of what you send where, when and what the editorial response is. At its simplest a single lined exercise book with numbered pages will suffice.

Number everything you write and make the book's right-hand pages into your manuscript records. When you despatch copy numbered 4 and titled 'Fishing in Galway', for instance, take page 4 of your book, top it with 'Fishing in Galway: 800 words' and detail, in columns if you wish, where you have sent it, the date of despatch and whether pix were included. Leave the last column for completion when you hear its fate; if accepted, a plain 'A' and the fee received are good to see when browsing through the book at a later date. If the copy does not sell the first time out you use the last column for its date of rejection – and start its second journey on the line below.

The clean left-hand pages are useful for making notes that do not readily fit into any preordained column, such as reminders of people's names and preferences, often elicited from contact with the magazine during negotiations about the copy. Here I also paper-clip letters from magazines relating to the copy on the right.

As you gain experience you will find not every piece of copy needs a page to itself so you simply draw a thick line below the successful history of one item before starting another. Your record keeping may develop into a more sophisticated routine but, however you decide to work and whatever system you choose, I urge you to keep it as straightforward as possible. It is never profitable to spend a disproportionate amount of time and effort keeping records, important as their safe keeping undoubtedly is.

The rewards

It is wise to keep your financial affairs in order by opening a special bank account solely for your earnings as a writer. This is regardless of any other accounts you may hold and will prove its value when the time comes to satisfy the tax inspector. Annual income-tax returns cannot get muddled up with any other sources of income you may have and you can, if necessary, demonstrate exactly what your earnings have been. If you also draw on this 'writing' account for your expenses you will benefit by being able to total them without difficulty, making sure you set the correct amount against your earnings in any tax year.

Tax

The Inland Revenue agrees that self-employed people who sell their services to a variety of customers are, in effect, without *regular* employment. They are therefore exempt from taxation at source under Schedule E or PAYE and can smooth any cash-flow problems by being assessed under Schedule D. This recognises that a percentage of overhead costs can be deducted from taxable income. Being allowed to pay tax in two instalments, usually at the beginning of January and July, is a further legitimate advantage.

Freelances regularly published by the same magazine (with a weekly children's column, monthly gardening tips and so on) can fall into a horrible no-man's-land between being taxed at source and being allowed the advantages of the Schedule D umbrella. If part of your work is regular, argues the Inland Revenue, you cannot be considered wholly freelance. Trying to sort out the complexities of being part employed and part freelance, partly taxed at source and partly taxed under Schedule D, is a nightmare as I know from bitter personal experience. Before you accept a 'regular' job check with the magazine's accounts department that you will always be paid gross, i.e. without deduction of tax or national insurance. (The horror is compounded when insurance contributions are also deducted and tax is levied at the maximum rate, disregarding personal allowances.) If you cannot be given such assurance, perhaps because the magazine, in good faith, fears pressure from the taxman and dare not commit itself to your cause, insist you will be informed if and when any changes occur in the way you are being paid. Should your Schedule D classification be withdrawn you will at least be able to decide whether the regular job in question will be worth doing if you continue.

All being well and even though you never meet nor expect to meet any problems about your freelance standing it is helpful to use headed paper carrying the word 'freelance' beneath or beside your name. Business cards should do the same. Some writers fear the word belittles their capabilities in the eyes of professional or staff journalists. Anyone who has worked on both sides of the fence knows it takes as much – if not more – hard work, determination and sheer *professionalism* to succeed as a freelance as it does to satisfy one's superiors in an editorial office where other people may cover for one's mistakes and shortcomings.

To strengthen your freelance status, spread your net wide. Write for as many magazines as you can in as many regions or countries as you can and in as many diverse ways as you can. This, you may enlighten the taxman should he ever query your status, is what freelancing is all about. And in case he doesn't know what the word originally meant you can remind him the first people to be called 'freelances' were mercenary knights and men-at-arms who roamed around Europe after the Crusades working for anyone who would employ them for what were usually short-term assignments. You may not carry a sword but you are a modern-day freelance and should be taxed as one.

Claiming expenses

There are a good many expenses you may legitimately claim to reduce your tax liability. I have been amazed to find that what is allowable may vary according to where you live and what experience your tax inspector has (or has not) of other writers or self-employed people. This being so (and should it *be* so?), it is best to be as clear as you can be about your own position when you establish your self-employed status.

You may rightly set against tax anything you buy for establishing and running your business as a self-employed writer. This may include the following, if relevant to your particular type of writing:

Postage
Accountancy fees
Office heating, lighting and cleaning
Fees for conferences and tutorials
Professional subscriptions

Business equipment (computer, word-processor, printer, etc.)
Printer and/or typewriter ribbons
Subscriptions to professional bodies or associations
Telephone and fax charges
Photocopying costs
Stationery (including printed paper, business cards, etc.)
Research costs
Books necessary for work
Insurance and maintenance of office equipment
Disks and tapes
Reference books (including this one)
Hotels
Travel expenses
Secretarial expenses

Amortising the purchase price of essential equipment such as a typewriter, a word-processor or a camera is usually allowable by negotiation with the tax inspector: subject to the capital cost this may work out in the first and second years at 20 per cent or 25 per cent of the purchase price, with perhaps smaller amounts allowed for subsequent years until the total sum has been defrayed.

If you do not want to make your tax inspector scoff you should be careful to keep your capital expenses in proportion to what you hope you will earn. This is particularly sensible before you are firmly established. Gaining a reputation for selling reliable work pleases more than editors: the Inland Revenue will also accept that you are a serious writer and that the claims you list to be set against tax are authentic.

It is permissible to offset so much against tax that you are actually working at a tax loss, a situation some writers are able to use to their benefit by setting a writing loss against income from other sources.

The seventeenth-century French politician Jean-Baptiste Colbert had a clear view of the situation: 'The art of taxation' he said, 'consists in so plucking the goose as to obtain the largest amount of feathers with the least amount of hissing.' But regardless of what we may sometimes believe, the Inland Revenue is not entirely without compassion. In assessing freelances with little or no income your tax inspector must be satisfied that you are working as a writer (researching, gathering material or engaged upon legitimate business, if not actually covering paper with words) with every intention of achieving publication. In such circumstances simple three-line statements will suffice and long detailed tax accounts are not required. Of course you must still keep careful records both for your own protection, should you ever wish to query Inland Revenue demands, and as evidence to support your claims against expenses, should substantiation be needed.

In times past freelances taxed under Schedule D were able to claim a proportion of their domestic rates as tax deductible. Such Inland Revenue largesse does not apply to the Council Tax, which charges more for business premises than for domestic. As a writer, whether employed in another sphere or not, you may claim that the room where you write is not exclusively a 'business' work room if it is also used for domestic purposes.

Even before you've earned anything from your writing you may legitimately claim expenses providing you have already informed the Inland Revenue that you are in business as a writer. For example, your work may take months or even years to research before a word of the finished product is written and you may carry forward a sum covering 'work in progress' for many years, although this is more likely to be the working pattern of book writers than magazine journalists.

Good record-keeping pays dividends. With it you needn't fear the shadow of the Inland Revenue while also being fair to your own pocket. Be meticulous in being able to produce genuine records and receipts to substantiate your writing credentials if you are ever asked to do so.

At the start of your writing career you may be tempted to dismiss the first few sums earned as not worth telling the Inland Revenue about. Think again! No matter how little you have earned the taxman must be told. And be encouraged to realise that it is in your interest to tell him: there might be awkward questions to answer if you don't, but when you do you are establishing a firm and honest base from which you will be able to claim expenses to set against tax in the future.

I like the story of the money that arrived at the Treasury accompanied by an unsigned note. It read: 'I can't sleep at night for thinking how I did not declare all my earnings five years ago and so did not pay the correct amount of tax. Please accept the enclosed £65. If I find I still can't sleep I'll send you the rest.'

The following book provides further useful information and is packed with help for everyone, even those folk who are not writers – 50 ways to save tax, easy steps to filling in your tax return, tax-efficient investments and lots of help for the self-employed are among the valuable contents:

Lloyds Bank Tax Guide by Sara Williams and John Willman, by Penguin Books Ltd., 27 Wrights Lane, London W8 5TZ. Tel: 071-416 3000. Worth every penny of the tax deductible £7.99 price.

Re-selling your copy

The thought of selling one piece of work to different editors causes panic in the hearts of many writers. Can this be done without incurring trouble? Don't editors mind? Is this syndication?

This is a summary of the position:

- Selling identical copy to different editors, i.e. posting off duplicates of what you've written to various magazines offering them the first chance of publishing the piece is – technically – impossible. You can only give one child the *first* lick of the lollipop. Offer First British Rights in a particular piece to more than one editor and you will not only be courting trouble, you will also be guilty of deception. Once first rights have been sold you cannot offer them to someone else.

- To re-sell your copy but still be able to offer first rights it must not be the same as what you have already sold. In this way you will not be selling the same piece. By rewriting your work for another market you are not deceiving or defrauding anyone. In fact you will be doing your writing experience a world of good.

  To a family-orientated magazine, for instance, I sold first rights in an article about researching family history. Then I rewrote my own copy for a publication dealing with developments in computer programming, this time slanting the article to the value of computer programs in such work. This second article was, of course, quite different from the first so it earned a whole new set of rights for itself and I was able to offer first rights to another editor. In fact all I had done was write a second article out of my own first article and additional research material I had already gathered. Call this process 'rewriting' or 'recycling' or 'adapting' or whatever you wish, but it is very different from the practice referred to in the first point.

Syndication

Syndication is a system that *does* permit multiple selling of the same piece of work for readers of different magazines – even at the same time. It works on the principle that they will not be the *same* readers because the essence of syndication is that circulation areas do not overlap. This effectively cuts national and nationally circulated magazines out of the syndication business and confines it to smaller, regional or local publications. In the newspaper world it can be profitable but in the magazine world it is often hardly worth bothering about. The exceptions to this generalisation lie in specialist copy written at the behest of syndication agencies, some of which deal exclusively with overseas syndication. Writers whose work is sufficiently well known may find advantages in such work but it is not an easy option. Can you write copy that will *without being edited* appeal to readers in, say, three or four different countries? When you're aiming to syndicate to the world the what-to-write-about problem is not easily solved. See also Writing in English in Chapter 7.

Training for the job

The majority of freelances working outside and even inside magazine offices have never been specifically trained for the job. So if you fall into this category, perhaps having taken up writing as an extra when working in a different full-time capacity or when in your retirement years, you are in good company. All the same you may wish to broaden your knowledge in the fascinating topic of writing for magazines. Such learning, though not essential, is never wasted.

Many official and semi-official courses for journalists are widely advertised in writers' publications. The best often require personal attendance, a disadvantage for some potential students, and the worst are little better than money-grabbers offering meaningless but high-priced credentials and a heap of old-hat advice.

For serious and worthwhile study you might investigate the National Vocational Qualification requirements and delve into basic topics such as layout, proofing, researching and general writing skills. The best tutors will be professional working journalists but freelance writers are generally welcomed as students, as are working and former magazine staffers. The National Vocational Qualification is not a method of training so much as a confirmation of abilities. Basic attainment levels are assessed by the Periodicals Training Council (the Newspaper Society does the same in the newspaper field) on seven levels of competence. These include carrying out routine research and originating ideas for magazine feature work, planning assignments, and the presentation and transmission of copy.

Are such qualifications as this worth striving for? The National Council for the Training of Journalists, who run the NVQ, is regarded by many magazine proprietors and publishers as virtually moribund and some of the working journalists queried on magazines and newspapers had never even heard of the NVQ. Several dismissed it as some wild scheme that failed to get off the ground a few years ago and others laughed it to scorn. So it's up to you.

I can't deny the benefits of formal post-graduate training in journalism have brought me many advantages: the greatest was being thrown in at the deep end and having to learn quickly. For that reason I urge you to take every chance in this writing business that comes your way. What you learn through doing the job will at the end of the day prove more valuable than formal training, should you have to choose between the two. Both will stand you in good stead in the future.

For more information you might like to contact the following:

National Union of Journalists, Acorn House, 314 Gray's Inn Road, London WC1X 8DP. Tel: 071-278 7916

British Association of Journalists, 97 Fleet Street, London EC4Y IDH. Tel: 071-353 3003. New trade union set up as a rival to the NUJ in 1992 by its sacked general secretary Steve Turner.

Correspondence courses

Correspondence courses for writers abound: are they worth paying for? The best are accredited to the Council for the Accreditation of Correspondence Colleges (Latton Bush

Centre, Southern Way, Harlow, Essex CN18 7BL. Tel: 0279 430009) which aims to maintain high standards. In the interests of readers thinking of indulging themselves I have made a close study of courses currently advertising their wares and have also contacted students, past and present, hearing their opinions, praise and complaints. In all cases discussed below I have been investigating only tuition offered in non-fiction and especially in relation to the writing of articles for magazines. I find a few correspondence courses are well established, the majority provide students with tuition and help but may fall short of the mark in several respects, and a few are – frankly – abysmal.

In the first category 'well established' usually means reliable at least in the sense of being honest and providing the service paid for. Unfortunately in some folks' minds 'well established' also has the connotation 'out of date'. It must be said I found such suspicions justified when I checked 'current marketing lists' from two major correspondence-course organisers. In one such list eight of the 25 recommended magazines had folded, seven of them more than a year earlier and a further two had moved to new addresses. Another list issued by a different 'well-established' correspondence course advised students, in 1992, to submit their work to (among other magazines) *Eve*, which was launched and died in 1973, *Everywoman* (which was merged into *Woman & Home* in 1966) and – almost unbelievably – *Home Chat* which passed away at the ripe old age of 63 way back in 1958.

In fairness I must report that courses run by two other companies quite unconnected with the first two take great pains to keep their marketing information as up to date as they can. They make the point (as anyone must and I do myself in this book) that the publishing of magazines is continually changing and students must learn to rely on their own market research to discover what is and is not being published at any given time, as well as what is and is not wanted by editors. All but two courses of this first type failed to supply details of their tutors' qualifications and experience and one told me I had 'no right' to seek such information.

Most of the courses I investigated fell in the middle range, being partly satisfactory but sometimes or in some respects of doubtful value. Their virtues include good attention to presentation, grammar, syntax and overall style and a noticeable emphasis on solving the problems of beginners. Exercises are set to cover a wide range of skills and, for the most part, are marked with care and at reasonable speed. On the debit side I found a general assumption that students enrolling at correspondence courses had received little or no instruction in these topics in their formal education; this could irritate those only seeking to improve their writing abilities.

Lastly, the *abysmal* category and that is not too strong a word to use. One course advised students to 'turn other people's work into freshly saleable material by altering a few words'. Another promises students free books to help with the tuition, not mentioning that two were published before 1960, and recommends markets of the same vintage: none of the free books has been updated since original publication and all have been unavailable in bookshops for several years.

And what about all that important guarantee most correspondence courses in writing dangle in front of their students' eyes? It goes something like this: *If you haven't earned enough to cover your fees by the time you complete the course we will refund the fees you have paid in full.* So do you get your money back if you are unsuccessful? My researches found only a proportion of the students enrolling, and paying, for a course complete it fully: note that vital point in the guarantee about *completing* the course. In no case did I find any time limit imposed in which the course(s) must be completed: indeed, quite the reverse. 'Take as long as you like', say the brochures. None of the organisers whose courses I delved into would discuss the percentage of non-finishers among their students within the past twelve months. All would have liked me to believe there were none – and no non-earners eligible to claim refunds either.

In view of such alleged success I had hoped my request for a list of students who have completed their courses and were now writing happily and selling well would have met with an eager response. With one notable exception, it didn't. The majority of the correspondence schools I contacted failed to respond on this point at all. 'We are bound by confidentiality', a few told me when a chance to publicise their worth and the achievements of their students might have been expected; odd, as every course brochure sent to prospective clients bulges with anonymous or 'initials only' testimonials.

That notable exception? In fairness I am happy to quote some of the praise several students offered me (*not* via the school concerned) without being under any obligation to do so. Fairness being a two-edged weapon, I also quote criticism obtained in identical circumstances:

The Writers' Bureau Ltd. Sevendale House, 7 Dale Street, Manchester M1 1JB. Tel: 061-228 2362. The courteous co-operation I received from the Principal included a list of tutors (with CVs), some of whom I know personally as excellent writers and teachers. Students report:

- 'They were efficient, concerned and particularly helpful when I needed advice on getting payment for a published article.'
- 'I am thrilled with the help and encouragement they have given me which has proved its worth many times in the fees received from magazines publishing work.'
- 'I found the written material uninteresting, flat and very basic but appreciate that it has been produced to cover a wide range of writing competence.'
- 'If I was struggling I would take offence at some of the literature they enclose with assignments.'

Potential students can only listen to the opinions of fellow writers and make up their own minds.

All work and no play?

When you write at home, whether in just a few snatched hours at the end of the day spent working elsewhere or as a part-time or full-time occupation, there is sure to come a day when you feel the need for contact with like-minded souls. Writing can be a solitary and lonely business, indeed it *must* be, for after all the reference books have been read and all the help and advice have been absorbed it comes down to what theatre-managers call BOS, bums on seats. The actual writing is only done by *sitting down and getting on with it*. Even writers collaborating on a project have to do their writing by themselves. The more you write the more you are likely to succeed but you will still be alone. A break among your own kind can work wonders for your confidence, your spirits and your future prospects. Do you need inspiration or encouragement? Maybe you'd find solace as well as enjoyment in joining a Writers' Circle.

Many freelances claim they found their true writing beginnings in Writers' Circles. Sharing a common interest often misunderstood by outsiders, their members are generally extremely friendly and keen to welcome newcomers. Yes, there are a few circles that seem to be the blind leading the blind amid an excess of mutual self-congratulation but it is always worth finding out what exists in your area and testing the waters. Failing that, how about starting one yourself . . . ?

The most comprehensive list of existing writers' groups is the *Directory of Writers' Circles* which may be obtained from Oldacre, Horderns Park Road, Chapel-en-le-Frith, Derbyshire SK12 6SY. £4.00 post free.

Apart from what many writers regard as their regular 'fix' of meeting fellow writers, there are many residential and non-residential schools and conferences where writers of all types gather to socialise and learn more of their craft. So numerous are they that I have space to mention only one – the largest, probably the oldest and certainly the best known. This is the *Writers' Summer School* held in rural Derbyshire for six days every August. Further details may be acquired from the Secretary: Philippa Boland, The Red House, Mardens Hill, Crowborough, Sussex TN8 1XN. Tel: 0892 653943.

Tenet insanabile multos scribendi cacoethes. Juvenal (AD 60–130)

'Many people have an incurable passion for writing.'

Index